CADILLAC
SEVILLE

Osprey AutoHistory

CADILLAC SEVILLE

Rear & front drive; diesel; 1975 on

THOMAS FALCONER

Published in 1984 by Osprey Publishing Limited
12–14 Long Acre, London WC2E 9LP
Member company of the George Philip Group

Sole distributors for the USA

Osceola, Wisconsin 54020, USA

British Library Cataloguing in Publication Data
Falconer, Thomas
    Cadillac Seville.—(Osprey autohistory series)
    1. Seville automobile
    I. Title
    629.2′222   TL215.C/
ISBN 0–85045–551–0

Editor Tim Parker
Associate Michael Sedgwick
Picture research by the author

Filmset in Great Britain
Printed in Spain by Grijelmo S.A., Bilbao

Contents

Cadillac background

It was a sunny afternoon in the Spring of 1953, the forthcoming Coronation of the young Queen Elizabeth II was on everyone's mind. In Cheltenham, England, a six year old boy was being pulled along by his mother, bored by a shopping trip to the Cavendish House department store and looking forward to an afternoon tea at the Cadena Café.

He was not looking where he was going, but his eyes were fixed on the steady stream of cars, dull and upright British saloons in endless blues and blacks on the tree lined Promenade.

Suddenly the little boy stopped dead in his tracks, refusing to let his mother drag him another inch. Tea would have to wait, for a vision was stopping at the traffic light beside him. It was white, as long as a lorry and as low as a speedboat, its driver in a state of rich red luxury unknown in a country where sugar was still rationed, with glittering gauges and pullable chrome knobs. In front the sweeping glass seemed to tell stories of adventure and speed; the side glass disappeared without even a frame in the front and rear doors.

The light changed to red, and the car dipped on its soft suspension, the driver chewed on his cigar. When the light changed to green, the back of the vast two-door dipped even lower and left the staid black and grey British saloons standing, a continuous gush of power uninterrupted by the familiar sound of gear changes, and on the boot lid,

Opposite *1904 model Cadillac with detachable tonneau. Things have begun*

7

between the fins like a jet aeroplane, the golden script 'Cadillac'. Up the hill, past the Queen's Hotel it disappeared, leaving the Promenade to conservative good taste.

Replenished with crumpets, chocolate cake and a glass of milk, the boy wanted to know how this vision of loveliness fitted into the ordinary pattern of things. 'Mummy, a Cadillac must be the best car in the world.' 'No, Tom, Rolls-Royce is the best car

Above *In 1908 the Dewar
Trophy was awarded by RAC
in London to Cadillac for
achieving 'interchangeability
through standardization of
parts'*

Left *The Dewar Trophy trial
of 1908 at Brooklands*

in the world.' 'Mummy, I think the Queen should
drive in a Cadillac' 'No, she drives in a Daimler and
anyway a Cadillac is not British!'

As children usually do, the small boy felt short-
changed by adult explanations and decided to
research the matter further. He also felt a particular
sympathy for the Queen, who in a year when
everything should be best for her, couldn't ride in
real luxury because she had to travel British.

Cadillacs continued to get more powerful V8s, and grew longer, lower and wider for another twenty years. Rolls-Royce kept the title of 'The Best Car in the World', not through how well they did things but through how well they were made. Daimlers just got duller: apart from a line of badge-engineered Jaguars, they also continued to make limousines for mayors or undertakers.

Yet when Cadillac launched a new compact formal four-door sedan called the Seville in 1975, it copied the slab sided Rolls-Royce Silver Shadow in so many ways that one began to wonder what had happened to American automotive aspirations. After a successful four-and-a-half year production

First mass production V8 engine for the 1915 models

run the Seville was changed completely, and this time it appeared with front-wheel-drive and an extraordinary swept tail not unlike the Queen's Daimler which had so failed to impress a six-year-old English boy 27 years earlier.

What had happened in those two decades to make Cadillac, the unquestioned style leaders of the fifties and early sixties, to go first to Europe for one model and then to the pages of European automotive history for the next?

Cadillac has a long and distinguished history. Of all the American manufacturers who have started up, merged or gone bust since the turn of the century only Cadillac, established in 1902 as a car

A 1934 V12 'two-passenger' coupé with concealed spare wheel

Right *The 1938 Sixty Special.*
Bill Mitchell's first design for
an owner-driver sporting
Cadillac

Left *The 1948 '62' Touring
Sedan marked the first
Cadillac with fins*

'Body drop'. It's 1950 and four door assembled shell about to be fitted at Clark Avenue. Does the '100,000' sticker mean what it suggests?

1950 '62' Coupé de Ville. A typical air brush half tone of the day

manufacturer has had the privilege of seeing its name became part of the daily language. Cadillac was and is synonymous with luxury and success in the world's largest English-speaking nation.

It is a measure, too, of the nature of industrial organization in the United States that Cadillac should have been for all but its first six years a division of General Motors, the world's largest manufacturing Corporation, rather than a small specialized company (such as Rolls Royce) marketing a very expensive product for the elite. Cadillac's founder, Henry M. Leland, entered the automotive field by building single cylinder engines for Oldsmobile, also later to become a GM division. At this time he traded as Leland and Faulconer: he started producing his own car in 1902 under the name Cadillac, after disagreements with Oldsmobile. His early success in supplying engines to Oldsmobile had been based on high precision engineering, and this continued to be the basis for their reputation. In the formative years until the First World War company success was immediate.

Cadillac was outstanding among early manufacturers for having a tightly controlled production operation, making all their own components to the exacting standards of Henry Leland. They were pioneers in a concept which is now taken for granted by both manufacturer and purchaser alike, that any component from one of their cars will interchange directly with the same component in another example of the same model. In practice this meant that engines and gearboxes, for instance, could be built up on a production line basis as an assembly operation, without any need for fitting and honing by craftsmen at each stage of assembly. From the customer's viewpoint, it meant that a single spare part would be sure to fit his car, and could be fitted by a comparatively unskilled mechanic with the minimum delay.

In 1908 Cadillac was awarded the RAC's prestigious Dewar Trophy in England, after three cars completed a trial in which they were completely stripped down to the last nut and bolt, and their component parts swapped round at random by the supervising judges. The cars were then reassembled and driven for 500 miles around the banked Brooklands circuit. This was particularly significant in England and its colonies, which would have no true mass production until after the First World War, and would be lucrative export markets for Cadillac who exported 15 per cent of total production. As a result of the award of the Dewar Trophy Cadillac adopted the 'Standard of the World' maxim which they have used ever since, though changed recently to 'Standard *for* the World' for legal reasons.

In 1910 Cadillac became the first manufacturer to introduce completely closed body styles available

17

off the showroom floor. In 1912 they pioneered electric self starters, lighting and ignition for which they were awarded a second Dewar Trophy, the first and only manufacturer in the world ever to win the award twice. The coil ignition and electric starting were the work of Charles Kettering and his Dayton Engineering Laboratories, later to become another GM Division, Delco.

In 1914 Cadillac dropped their four cylinder engine in favour of a 90 degree side valve V8 for the 1915 model year, thus making Cadillac the first manufacturer with a V8 in true volume production. It remains to be seen whether they will also be the last US manufacturer to make one.

In 1923 they pioneered an inherently balanced V8 with compensated crankshaft followed in 1928 by

A 1956 Eldorado Seville, the first Cadillac to use the 'Seville' name. It was the hardtop version of the Biarritz luxury convertible

safety glass as standard and a clash-proof synchromesh transmission. Still developing engines, Cadillac made the first series production V16, a 45 degree V engine with overhead valves and hydraulic tappets. Later, in 1934, Cadillac became the first American manufacturer to conceal the spare wheel within the bodywork.

In 1938 a new smaller Cadillac was introduced, the Sixty Special, definitely not for chauffeur drive, and with styling that was a breakthrough; for the first time the trunk was fully integrated into the smooth form of the body with the roof sitting distinctly and separately on the top of this long form. It had no running boards, and the window detailing resembled that of contemporary convertibles. But of particular significance was that this was the youthful Bill Mitchell's first styling

The 1960 Eldorado Seville changed the image a lot. It looks lower, sleeker and longer. The fins are deadly

exercise for Cadillac. Mitchell's name must inevitably be linked with all new Cadillac designs from this one until the introduction of the new front-wheel-drive Seville, because he was chief of the Cadillac's studio from 1936 till 1949, and then he headed the whole G M Styling section until 1978. He took over this position from Harley Earl, the first stylist ever employed by GM, who came to them from a coachbuilding firm in California. His first assignment was to style the La Salle, Cadillac's less expensive line. Its launch, unfortunately, came shortly before the recession, and a subsequent cost cutting exercise in 1934, even gave it an engine from Oldsmobile Division, as well as various other off-the-shelf GM parts. The La Salle was a limited success, and even 40 years later this experiment cast an influence on the size, naming and price structure

*Big contrast, a 1971 Eldorado
8.2 litre convertible
photographed in England.
Rear wing grilles echo those on
early fifties cars; see page 16*

of the new smaller Cadillac.

World War Two finished off most of the effective
opposition to Cadillac in the luxury car field, and
they remained virtually unopposed in terms of sales
volume by either Chrysler's Imperial, sometimes a
technically superior car, Packard or Lincoln. The
latter had been founded by Henry Leland in 1917,
after he quit Cadillac following an argument with
GM chief Durant, a pacifist who had refused to
allow Leland to build Liberty aircraft engines.

Cadillac were first with fins in 1948, starting a
higher and wider battle which lasted until the
fabulous 1959 model, the same year that Cadillac
first fitted cruise control and Guidematic automatic
dipping headlights.

A new overhead valve engine, introduced for the
1949 season, powered a Coupé De Ville to a tenth
place at Le Mans in 1950. Entered by sportsman
Briggs Cunningham, it earned Cadillac a new

respect in the eyes of European enthusiasts.

Cadillac offered front-wheel-drive on the Eldorado two door coupé in 1967, sharing the technology with Oldsmobile who had introduced the same system on their Toronado a year earlier. They steadily increased the size of its engine until 1970, when at 500 cu. in. (8.2 litres) it was the largest in the industry. Fuel consumption was suffering accordingly; the author's 1971 Eldorado convertible simply would not improve on 10mpg, even gently driven on a long run; that's an awful lot of petrol.

The 1973–74 fuel crisis and subsequent shortages affected motor manufacturers worldwide. It was a boon for some, particularly those manufacturers of small to medium size machines with an established dealer network in the United States; but a potential disaster for others, perhaps none more so than Cadillac.

The three 1908 single-cylinder cars entered for the Dewar Trophy attained a mean of 29.64mpg, while the V8 introduced for 1915 averaged only 12mpg. No Cadillac would do much better than this until 1975.

Overnight, a policy of larger, heavier and therefore thirstier was shown to be an awful mistake, dealers saw themselves facing ruin, and the 'Standard of Excellence', the ultimate symbol of success, was starting to look like a gas guzzling monster. Even worse, its driver, was seen as a man with no feeling for the now fashionable environment.

Cadillac had to have a smaller car. It is to their lasting credit that they did not dress up a Chevy Nova with leather and power seats, as is still sometimes suggested by writers who should know better. They instead created a car which was unique, and has become a four door classic in its own time.

The new Seville

The Seville was launched into a surprised world on Tuesday 22 April 1975, and created an unprecedented amount of interest. *Car and Driver* ran a nine page comparative road test with a Rolls-Royce Silver Shadow in its June issue, while *Motor Trend* had featured the car on the cover in May, with a seven-page preview by Karl Ludvigsen.

The press had every reason to be excited because Cadillac had never before introduced a compact model. The big city dailies were interested because the car was clearly going to be more economical and this story about a smaller Cadillac had to be news—almost a man-bites-dog story.

The car magazines were interested because it was obvious that this new Cadillac was going to be lively and better handling. Cadillac's marketing department, led by Gordon Horsburgh, had obviously done an excellent job drumming-up interest in the car's development.

One of the first press stories originated with the *Chicago Sun Times* in October 1974. It suggested that the car would be called the La Salle, and would feature a fuel injected V8 engine, four wheel disc brakes, and an anti-skid system. The Mercury Monarch and Ford Granada (US version) had already been promoted as the American answers to the Mercedes-Benz 280, and now it was suggested the new La Salle would be the American Rolls-Royce and look a lot like it.

A further leak to UPI on 6 February 1975, said

the car would be called Seville after the city in the south-west of Spain, and admitted that the name La Salle had been dropped because of the lingering stigma attached to Cadillac's earlier companion make. Since Ford had launched their luxury compact Granada, and Chrysler their rival Cordoba, it was quickly pointed out that Spanish names were all the rage. In fact, Seville had also been the name of the luxury version Eldorado offered from

Cadillac employees get a sneak preview of the 'International in Size' new car prior to a six week 'furlough' for model changeover. Released to the press 7 February 1975, teasers like this kept up interest

April 1975; the first 2000 Sevilles were all silver with silver vinyl roofs. The upright back window and the lower moulding line of the vinyl roof cleverly reflect the styling of the Rolls-Royce Silver Shadow

Two new LaSalles are presented in the 1940 Cadillac line, a standard and special. The two series have frontal resemblance, but differ in bodies, passenger compartments and appointments. Increased room, greater comfort and reduced operating costs have been made possible by new design and chassis improvements. Above is the touring sedan in the LaSalle Special series.

Last of the La Salles, this one a 1940 Four Door Special. Cadillac called it a touring sedan

1956 through 1960 as the hardtop equivalent of the Biarritz convertible.

Bill Mitchell knew exactly what was needed for the new car, 'the idea of the Seville was to get a reminiscence of the old 1938 Sixty Special, a sporty, more youthful Cadillac'.

Cadillac were determined to win back the sales that were being lost to Mercedes-Benz, and they established their design parameters with American Mercedes buyers in mind. It had to be a four door, it had to look more like an import but still retain a Cadillac flavour. Handling and driveability had to be better than a full-size Cadillac's. The master stroke, however which spelt ultimate success for the new Seville, was the decision to price it above its larger and heavier stable mates, a real reversal of Detroit tradition and the only sure way to equate smallness with desirability. Although the car was obviously smaller, it was always referred to as 'international' in size. The most important requirement of all was that the car should have the ride and interior silence of a Cadillac.

The car was in the 1600 Cadillac dealers' showrooms on 1 May, and all the examples were identical, the first 2000 finished in metallic silver, with matching leather interiors and padded 'Tuxedo Grain' vinyl roofs. Twelve-page brochures exclusive to the Seville, with a plain white cover and 'Seville by Cadillac' printed in silver on the outside, were handed out by dealers.

Were Cadillac distancing themselves from the Seville with the preposition 'by', as though they were only the father and not the mother? When the Cimarron, featuring the ubiquitous 'J' chassis-body structure, was introduced in 1982 it was also known as a 'Cimarron by Cadillac' and featured in neither the 1982 or 1983 mainstream Cadillac catalogues.

Dealers had already been sent an exclusive Seville parts catalogue which listed, with special symbols, interchangeability with either other Cadillacs or other GM lines, so that spares could be located quickly if new owners should have trouble. Dealers also received two extra publications from the public relations department, one was a 130-page book of reprints from newspapers and magazines entitled 'Cadillac Seville Attracts World News Spotlight'. The other ran to 24-pages, was beautifully produced on glossy paper, and outlined the salient facts on Mercedes, Volvo, Rolls-Royce, BMW and Jaguar, so that dealers could aquaint themselves fully with their rivals in the market place.

All Sevilles were and are automatic; the information band is the dark strip at top of the dash. The power seats are very comfortable

Above *Power windows and window lock, door handle and luxuriously hinged, solid door-pull make the top panel. The lower panel has the six-way power seat, power door locks switch, manual door lock lever and remote mirror adjuster*

Right *The fully carpeted boot, including lid, has the already small capacity further reduced by a carpet covered, canister inflated spare wheel. The fuel filler is behind the hinged licence plate. Note the temporary strut holding the lid open on this prototype shot!*

Above *1975–76 cars have white lens parking lamps; the cornering lamp lights the side of the road at night when the direction indicator is activated*

Opposite *Deep stainless mouldings at the lower sides of the car give the right design poise and emphasize the large 15 in. wheels. Like Mercedes-Benz and Rolls-Royce, the new Seville has short front and long rear overhangs. The Spanish, or rather Spanish Colonial, background emphasized the origin of the name. Seville is in southern Spain; Cadillac is a small town in south-west France and the family name of the discoverer of the city of Detroit*

Looking at that brochure now, it is apparent that the new car fell down technically in two areas. It was the only one with rear leaf springs and the only one with rear drum brakes. In every other way the new Seville measured up very well indeed: a fuel-injected engine, automatic air conditioning, automatic level control and a long list of standard features.

Bill Mitchell has been quoted as saying 'Nobody's buying Mercedes for looks'. He was determined that looks alone should sell the Seville; thus the design that he and his assistants came up with in the Cadillac Advanced Studio at the GM Teck Centre has become a classic.

Early designs had had Hooper Daimler overtones, which were to reappear in 1980, and the engineers had certainly been keen to incorporate front-wheel-drive and independent rear suspension; but the 1973–74 fuel crisis had meant the speeding up of development, and further design studies were

The Seville would have been hooked down to the floor to give this 'low look' studio shot. Self-levelling rear suspension ensures that the car always rides higher than this

based on the X-bodied G M Chevrolet Nova.

It must, however, be emphasized that the Seville was then developed to a stage where it was very much a car in its own right, built by Cadillac on its own production line with its own sheet metal.

Even at the time of its launch, no one was really sure how much X-body was incorporated, some thought there was the boot lid, others the doors or even the whole floor pan. The only sure way to find out was by cross-checks on the parts book. The truth is that the complete front subframe, the rear subframe cross members and the rear compartment floor pan were borrowed from the other X-bodied cars. No other major body parts were, however, from this source.

Before the launch of the Seville a cadillac was a rather special kind of car. It is the ultimate refinement of all those qualities that mean absolutely nothing to sports car enthusiasts. In its dynamic functions it is barely adequate, with under-damped suspension, lazy steering response, limited rear suspension travel, inadequate sideways support from the seats, and excessive weight leading to poor acceleration and braking.

But the things it does well it does brilliantly, giving it a tremendous appeal to a non-enthusiast market, and convincing the already converted at the same time. If your other car is a Corvette or a Porsche, or you drive a Peterbilt truck for a living, the appeal of the Cadillac is tremendous. You press the door handle button, and both front door key holes are illuminated and the interior lights have lit before you open the door. The door opens wide and high, and shuts with the lightest pressure but with reasuring firmness. The driver's seat has six-way power control, even the shortest driver can have a commanding view of the road ahead. The seats are high and wide, with individual centre arm rests to give an armchair driving position. A small steering

On the street Sevilles always stand out. Often lovingly maintained by their proud owners

wheel tilts and telescopes to give a full range of adjustment, and springs up and forward to release even the most portly driver. Electric window switches and lockout, power door locks, and mirror adjustment are all in a panel on the inner driver's door, while other controls are set in their own plastic, chromium-surrounded simulated wood panel. No aircraft style switch gear here. A chime urges you to fasten your seatbelt, and starting is instantaneous. There is no tachometer, nor any instruments except a speedometer and fuel gauge.

The powerful and fully automatic temperature control heating and air conditioning can be set to the desired internal temperature. There is no need to select heater or air conditioning mode; the desired temperature can be maintained summer or winter. On the road the car is ideal for enjoying the four speaker stereo radio with its self seeking facility. Not for the Cadillac owner the burble of exhaust or hum of tyres; instead he can relax in gentle conversation with cosseted passengers, or the delights of stereo in one of the most acoustically ideal environments on wheels.

For the urban motorist who will probably fly the long trips anyway, the early Seville is the kind of car that is a pleasure to use daily, a pleasure to get in and out of, always relaxed and unfussed, with a commanding driving position: short enough to park, and always relaxing to drive. Added to all this, it looks distinguished—the understated elegance of success.

Like the Jaguar XJ6, the new Seville was dominated by its wheels. They were pulled right to the outside edge of the round wheel arches to give the car stance and poise, to emphasize that this, like the old Sixty Special, was a driver's car. Cadillac chief engineer Robert Templin had insisted on 15 in. wheels, and Mitchell who always wanted 'wider treads', went along with him. He recalled discussing the design of the Jaguar XJ6 saloon with Sir William Lyons at the London Motor Show. He had asked about the effect of gravel with this design, and Lyons replied 'That doesn't bother us, a little gravel shows you're driving the car!' The sides were plain, with a flute running along the top and into the sides of the boot, and a single plain moulding between the wheel arches which were themselves emphasised with further bright trim.

The front and rear federal side marker lamps were cleverly incorporated into the parking lamps, which wrapped round each corner, avoiding the messy appearance of separate afterthought installations found on the American versions of all the imports which Cadillac had already identified as its targets. The headlamps, parking lamps and grille were all neatly integrated below a flat bonnet carrying the Cadillac script and crest, and above a heavy plain bumper with rubber impact strip and small overriders flanking additional air intake grilles. The doors had full window frames to ensure silence at speed, and there was a formal roof line with a very upright back window. The roof was covered in cushioned vinyl, with a subtle treatment of the curve where this met the main body.

Unlike any of its European rivals, the Cadillac had the usual GM-style concealed windscreen wipers which contributed to the smooth and uncluttered lines. The rear deck was plain and steeply sloped and the underbody swept up sharply as well, to give a neat little rear panel over a plain rear bumper with a black impact strip. This looked great, but gave the Seville a very small boot, which then had to accommodate the space-saver spare wheel. Its European rivals all managed to accommodate a full size spare without loss of boot space. Final external dimensions compared directly with those of the Mercedes-Benz 450SE.

On the road the new Seville gave a sound level of

66dB at 70mph, making it unquestionably the quietest car in the world at that time. · This extraordinary silence at speed was a result of a great deal of painstaking effort by Cadillac engineers, and a remarkable achievement considering the use of many standard GM components.

To keep road noise out of the car, extensive use had been made of computer analysis. The front subframe was finally mounted on six Isoflex

1976 model front and rear elevations. There's that bold honeycomb front grille and those engraved rear lenses

mountings, which were softer in their fore and aft plane than laterally and vertically. Conventional Delco shock absorbers were then used to damp this fore and aft movement; these were attached at their upper ends to the front inner wings. The rear springs were fitted with Teflon inter liners, and the rear joint in the drive shaft was of constant velocity rather than conventional type.

Very soft weather strips (expensive to replace)

were used all around the doors. A hydraulic damper was incorporated in the steering to reduce kickback of the wheel, so inclusive of the four dampers in the energy absorbing bumpers there were no less than eleven hydraulic shock absorbers on the car. Rear suspension was self-levelling with air springs incorporated in the rear shock absorbers controlled by an engine vacuum powered pump and height sensor of a type already in use in other Cadillac models.

Cadillac had started out by supplying engines to Oldsmobile at the turn of the century. Now, having no small V8 themselves they had to buy Oldsmobile's cast iron 350 of oversquare dimensions; and gave it ten extra bhp with electronic fuel injection for each cylinder. This engine had originated in the early 1960s, and would subsequently prove strong enough to convert into a diesel. Transmission was by a shortened version of the Turbo Hydramatic 400 unit, the same gearbox as used by Rolls-Royce, but with a conventional column mounted lever rather than the Rolls' superb electric control.

For the driver, a plain matt black trim at the very top of the dash board lit up with warning lights when the ignition was turned on. This 'information band' included two fuel economy lights, a 'trunk open' light and even a 'level ride' light which showed when the self-levelling had done its job. The driver's seat had six way power as standard; this was optional on the front passenger seat, which had manual recline. Power recline was optional on both seats. The inertia reel seat belts were designed to release their tension once pulled out to the desired length, and only wound themselves back up again when signalled to do so by a switch connected to the door.

If the driver was leaving his car parked in the city he could twist the lever behind the headlamp switch to turn on the 'twilight sentinel'. This would automatically bring on his parking lights at dusk, and his headlights when he turned his ignition switch. He could also leave his headlights on long enough to reach his front door when he got home.

So that he knew that all his light bulbs were working properly, fibre optic cables, (as previously used on 1968–71 Corvettes) led from each bulb to displays on the top of each front wing, and inside the top of the back window which could be seen in the mirror. An am/fm signal seeking radio with front and rear speakers was standard equipment and there was the further option of an eight-track tape player built into the radio. On the road, the Seville would do about 115mph and 18 miles per Imperial gallon at a steady 70mph.

Cadillac Division's general manager Edward C. Kennard congratulates Joe Krupik, an assembly worker since the Second War as the 5 millionth postwar Cadillac, a '76 Seville, comes off the line in April 1976

45

Rear-wheel-drive

For the 1977 model year a number of changes were made, the most significant in the history of the rear wheel drive car.

The front grille changed from a bold eggcrate to a more subtle vertical 35-fin design, in line with other Cadillac models of the year. This new idiom was accentuated by an upper moulding on the lifting part of the bonnet lid, which had the Cadillac script engraved on it. This replaced the separate script which was previously fixed immediately above the left-hand headlamp. The white lenses of the twin front indicator and parking lamps were replaced by amber lenses, an unfortunate change which broke up the well integrated front elevation of the earlier cars. At night, of course, all the front parking lamps show amber because amber bulbs were used in the earlier cars. The cornering lamps remained white.

For the driver, there was a new steering wheel which still obscured the information band, though it abandoned the large fake wood disc in the middle of the horn push. The wheel was still colour co-ordinated with the rest of the interior.

Mechanically, the good news was that rear disc brakes were at last available, using a similar but smaller caliper and pad to that on the front.

The parking brake continued to be foot operated by a pedal on the left side of the steering wheel, complete with its vacuum powered release linked to the gear selector lever. Cadillac claimed this sytem gave a true auxiliary brake since the ratchet was not operational when the engine was running and the car in gear or neutral. The effect of the new rear disc brakes could be perceived from the driving seat when driving hard, and the Seville became the first Cadillac with this feature, even if this was twenty years after they had been available on some British cars.

The 1977 sales brochure described the suspension

1977 Seville with new grille, painted roof and optional wire wheel disc covers

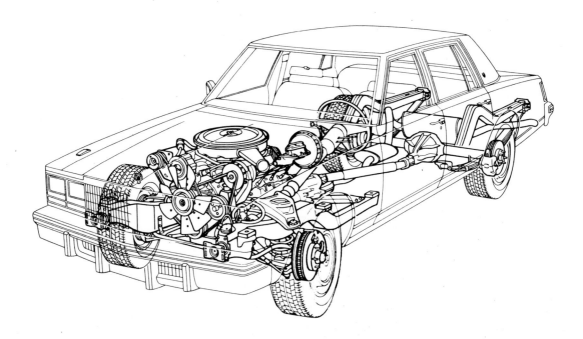

*Cutaway view of 1977–79
Seville showing ventilated
rear disc brakes, two silencers
and separate front and rear
sub frames*

system as having been 're-tuned', but Cadillac had actually done away with the clever hydraulic dampers between the front sub-frame and body, and had stiffened up the isoflex mountings, improving the handling without spoiling the ride.

The air conditioning was also improved to make it more economical. Since its introduction, the Seville had always had an 'economy' position which allowed the air conditioning pump to be disengaged with its electric clutch to save as much as 2mpg. The system was now further refined so that the compressor only engaged when necessary for cooling when the control was in the air conditioning automatic mode. The signal seeking stereo was also improved by the addition of a scan button which enabled the driver to sample each station for six seconds automatically, locking on to the desired station by a second push of the button.

The optional cruise control was improved with the addition of a resume and advance switch. The 1977 cruise control system used a sensor in the speedometer head rather than the gear unit half way up the speedometer cable used on the earlier cars. After setting the desired cruising speed with the button on the end of the direction indicator stalk, this was held constantly until the brake pedal was touched, the brake light switch being used to cancel the cruise control. The resume position took the car back to the previously held speed, while the advance switch gently increased speed till released. Seville enthusiasts quickly accustomed themselves to the system using it on even the shortest journeys. The system reduces fatigue and leg and back ache, caused by constant muscular tension of the right leg when using the foot operated accelerator control.

'Authentic' chrome wire wheels by Dunlop of England required inner tubes; the wheels needed to be secured with McGard anti-theft nuts

Top left *1977 New York Motor Show. A special Seville was exhibited in two-tone brown with body colour hub caps. It was called simply 'Elegante'*

Bottom left *1977 Chicago Motor Show. Another, this time in two-tone black and grey with the darker colour uppermost (almost the production model) but now named 'La Espada'. The New York 'Elegante' was there too, but with wire wheels*

Above *1977 Geneva Motor Show. A third production forerunner. All in one colour, cream with lower side moulding and 'Seville Elegante' script behind front wing. Note that all these show cars have 'General Motors' scripts on moulding behind the front wheel, and smaller rear windows*

The production Elegante had two-tone paintwork divided by a full length brushed chrome strip, and a special interior. Authentic wire wheels were standard. This is a prototype shot, all but a few early production Elegantes had the same side rubbing strip as the standard car

Another option, attached to the drivers door mirror, was a rotary illuminated outside thermometer, particularly useful for warning of the possibility of ice. A digital display radio (incorporating a digital clock) was offered for the first time. When this feature was ordered, the clock display panel in the centre of the dash was blanked off with Seville script.

Cadillac had offered a power trunk lid on various models since 1962. This was introduced as a Seville option in 1977, pulling the lid shut when it was within an inch or so of its closed position. On all Sevilles, opening of the lid is remotely controlled via a release button inside the passenger's glove compartment.

Power operated sun roofs with a metal panel, and Astro roofs with a glass panel had become available during the 1976 model year, and were offered again in 1977. They were not installed at the factory, but fitted by a specialist in Detroit. Another new option was a painted metal roof to match the body colour, though the padded vinyl roof remained standard. The broad moulding round the rear window was left with its joints exposed, and painted body colour.

Above *Ms. Mimi Abel of Coral Gables, FL, receives the keys to the first limited edition Gucci Cadillac from Dr. Aldo Gucci himself*

Top left *The prettiest of all the modified Sevilles was the San Remo Ultima convertible from Westlake in Southern California, always one of the Seville's strongest sales areas. The car is two-door*

Bottom left *The Pierre Cardin Seville featured two-tone paint and wood grained stripe which could, in fact, be applied to any car in the Cadillac range*

Grandeur Opera Coupé; the owner of such a car would probably have fake propellors on his executive jet!

1978 studio pictures showing opera lamps and rear bumper underriders, and full width rear accent stripe

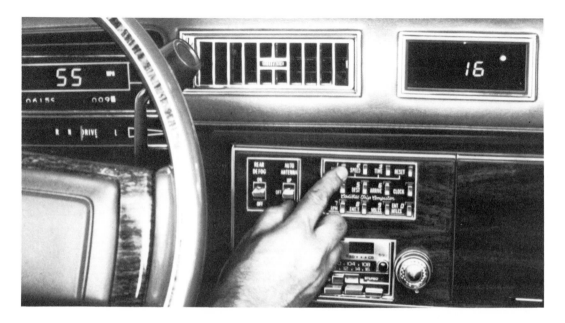

Mid-1978 trip computer meant that Seville was now available with a tachometer!

With this option, the car loses some of its essential style, since the rear quarter shows a marked similarity with the much cheaper, and larger Chevrolet Caprice. The loss of style was, however, accompanied by the loss of a corrosion point; vinyl roof Sevilles tend to rust at the lower edge seam.

For 1978 the obvious external difference was at the rear of the car; the winged emblem on the tail lights was in solid chromium, and the rear bumper had a pair of small vertical overriders below the rubber protector strip. The paint accent stripes were now carried right over the boot lid.

A more subtle change was that the impact strip along the doors of the front wing between the wheel openings now had a body colour inset. Two new options were available for the standard car. The first of these consisted of opera lamps on the 'C' pillars, in lieu of the Cadillac wreath emblem. Each contained a three amp white bulb and glowed white whenever the car lights were in use. Quite why they should be called opera lamps is obscure. They first appeared on Cadillacs in 1971. Lincoln called their similarly-located oval windows opera windows, an even more obscure use of the word, since these were the only windows on the sides of these cars that were inoperable!

Another new option was authentic chromed wire wheels, made in England for Cadillac by Dunlop. There was already a choice of three covers for the standard steel wheel; the standard full type with fine indentations around the rim, the turbine cover with pronounced radial fins around its perimeter, and the spoked wheel cover which could be immediately distinguished from the authentic wire wheel by its much larger centre. The new unit came complete with a set of four locking wheel nuts made by McGard of Buffalo, New York; the adapter key was permanently secured to the

There were more 1978s built than any other year

A typical 1978 model with Tuxedo Grain roof and wire wheel covers

wheel brace with a braided wire. Since they would fit virtually all General Motors cars except for the very smallest, the owner was well advised to protect them. At nearly $450 each in 1983 they are worth protecting. As on any wire wheels, broken spokes can be replaced with new ones supplied by Cadillac as off-the-shelf parts. A locking kit is also available for the simulated wire wheel covers, but these cost less than a third of the price of the authentic type to replace.

These same wire wheels formed the basis for the 'Elegante' model on which they were standard. The French word 'd'Elegance' had been used for some time for the De Ville series car in it's special edition guise, so it was logical that the Spanish 'Elegante' be applied to the Seville. It had duo-tone paintwork with a black top and silver bottom halves; it was also offered in saddle and brown. A full-length brushed chromium moulding extended along both sides, with a paint stripe below. Early Elegantes came without the lower body side moulding along the middle of the doors, which made them look rather slab sided, so this was quickly reintroduced. Elegante script was affixed to each 'C' pillar; opera lamps were not available.

Inside, the Elegante had perforated leather seating areas. Instead of the standard front seats with their twin armrests a single centre console divided the driver and passenger, with a large central armrest, writing 'desk' with lid, and space for an in car telephone, all lit with an interior lamp. The front seats on the Elegante incorporated pockets for the rear passengers.

Repeated for 1978 were the power-seat recliner for driver and passenger. The Seville passenger seat had had a manual recline lever since its introduction. Nash had been vilified in the early 1950s for their layback seats, which were thought to be contributing to the immorality of America's youth.

Introduced in April 1975, the first 2000 1976 Sevilles were painted all silver. Here's a publicity shot which shows nothing but says it all

Top left *Cadillac's marketing department expected great sales for the new downsized Caddy to the Pacific States. Plain and simple; one of the first 2000 '76s*

Bottom left *Cadillac luxury. Leather seats and shag pile carpeting came in 1976. All colour coded and deep*

Above *The 1977 model Seville (obviously) changed colour and had a new moulding capping for the finer toothed radiator grille. More elegant wheel discs, too, on this version*

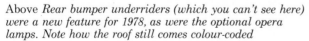

Above *Rear bumper underriders (which you can't see here) were a new feature for 1978, as were the optional opera lamps. Note how the roof still comes colour-coded*

Right *1979 was the last year for rear wheel drive. Cadillac constantly implied tradition and quality; witness the building behind this car with the wheel disc option*

Above *The 1979 Cadillac
Seville Elegante came with
the ladies, unlike the
aftermarket limited edition
Gucci (for an extra $7000)
which came with the
matching Gucci luggage
instead*

Right *1980 and the 'bustle
trunk'. The new Seville was
both quieter and roomier than
before inspite of its as
standard diesel engine. The
inspiration for that tail is
obvious and a master stroke
for Cadillac*

Above *The 1981 Cadillac Seville (this model's an Elegante) came with the variable displacement 6.0 litre engine. Some found the engine a handicap*

Left *The 82s had the 4.1 litre aluminium blocked V8 as standard, the diesel engine (in improved form) remaining as an option. Another factory press shot*

Above *The interior again; another 1983 Seville Elegante. Compare this with the shot of the 1976 car earlier. Many love this car*

Right *Finer radiator grilles were introduced for 1983 (another Elegante), front parking lights had white lenses again. Note the change of emphasis of Seville over Cadillac*

As a result, it was another 20 years before American cars came with adjustable seat backs. The HEI distributor was given electronic rather than direct vacuum control for its advance and retard.

The vacuum operated self levelling system for the rear suspension was replaced by a system using an underbonnet mounted twelve volt compressor and electronic height sensor at the rear axle.

In March 1978 the 350 cubic inch diesel was introduced as the first move towards a policy standardizing this type of engine power plant, and this makes a chapter all to itself. For 1979, the Seville carried on more or less exactly as before. Externally, it is possible to tell the difference from a 1978 because the right hand mirror glass is convex, not flat. Inside, fake burled walnut replaced fake rosewood on the fascia and door control areas, and a new steering wheel, with 'twenty minutes to four' spokes, gave a better view of the dash.

The diesel was now available from the beginning of the model year as was the optional trip computer, another mid-season option from 1978. This ingenious device operated much like a calculator, with a twelve button keyboard and three digital readouts. The first readout displayed speed, in place of the standard pointer speedometer. The second was a fuel gauge displaying the number of gallons of fuel remaining in the tank. The third display gave the input as it was entered on the keyboard, and then displayed the answer as on a calculator.

At various times during the Seville's history, Designer Editions have been offered, particularly by Gucci and Pierre Cardin. These were not originated by Cadillac themselves but by dealers, usually on a regional basis. The Pierre Cardin edition was offered by dealers in the north eastern states during 1979, and was applied to the whole Cadillac line. The side panels were painted out with free-standing contrasting panels of a hue darker than the main panel's, and without a moulding trim. The whole affect was rather unsatisfactory, though the Master presumably gave his assent.

Braman Cadillac in Miami were licensed by the Gucci organization to produce the Gucci edition, which inevitably came with a set of Gucci luggage, the only thing to be seen with at fashionable hotels in the late 1970s. This was soft luggage with sewn-round straps of red and green, and a Gucci badge on the front lid. Other significant details on the Gucci Seville were a retrimmed interior and Gucci badges and fabric for the vinyl roof. More than 200 of the cars were produced.

The dealers who had ordered and were selling these designer editions had realized something

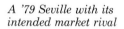

A '79 Seville with its intended market rival

which perhaps Cadillac had not, that the Seville had a tremendous appeal to lady drivers. The annual brochures always depicted women as passengers in cashmeres, pearls or furs, demonstrating the seductive charm of the reclining passenger seat or the fingertip lightness of the rear compartment reading-lamp switch. These *Vogue* readers were, however, buying the car because it was chic, easy to park, and had four doors and a power operated trunk lid for loading the loot from Bloomingdales. Even four years after production was finished, Cadillac dealers still report a strong demand for low mileage examples for female buyers, many of whom are on their second or third Seville.

The 1979 Elegante, now with its lower side moulding

Front-wheel-drive

If the 1975–79 model was pure and classical, with almost European restraint, then the new 1980 version was flashy, derivative, glamorous and romantic.

After just four and a half years of production and only one significant styling change—that only to the radiator grille surround—Cadillac now abandoned the pure and timeless form of the first series Seville and redesigned the car in every detail. Overstated opulence replaced understated elegance.

In remaining unchanged for four and a half years, the Seville was being treated as an exception to the normal policy of the annual update. Indeed, while the average American schoolboy with an interest in cars can probably identify any year of Firebird or Caprice at a glance, there are very few anywhere who can tie either series of Seville down to a specific year. With the Seville, the annual changes are very slight, but the differences are listed in these pages and summarized in the appendix.

The annual model change is a well established Detroit tradition, which persuades affluent America to change its twelve-month-old car after only a tenth of its useful life. It has been said of the full size body Cadillacs that they start their lives with doctors or dentists, and get moved on to restaurant managers and end up in the ghetto, giving good service in all three locations. Particularly through the 1950s and 1960s, Cadillac led the field in its spectacular annual model changes, vying with Chrysler in styling, and leaving the conservative end of the super luxury market to Lincoln with their old-fashioned, slab sided Continental. The Cadillac owner did not have to change his car for the new one with a different appearance and mechanical improvements, but if he chose to keep it for seven years and 100,000 miles the only difficulty or discomfort that he might experience would be the

The abandoned sloped back prototype for the first Seville; an idea revived once Cadillac felt it had hit out at Rolls-Royce and Mercedes-Benz

'Bustle trunk'; the new 1980 Seville, the then most controversial new model of the year. This is the Elegante version with optional simulated wire wheel covers

discovery that his cook would probably be enjoying and driving the same model.

Cadillac, more than any other GM car apart from Chevrolet's fibreglass bodied Corvette, is assembled with great attention to durability and resistance to corrosion, and is possibly the longest-lasting General Motors car. The use of numerically low rear axle ratios reduces stress on engines and transmissions, and the soft suspension gives the sprung part of the car an easy life.

There was probably no real styling justification for dropping the rear-wheel-drive Seville at the end of the 1979 model year. In fact, the De Ville and Fleetwood Brougham series cars were restyled to look remarkably like the old Seville with a very similar frontal treatment. The real motive for the change was to achieve front-wheel-drive independent rear suspension and rationalization of production.

Front-wheel-drive cars need convex dishing for

their wheels and a new body was required that gave them less emphasis. A concave dish wheel emphasizes the tyre while the convex wheel emphasizes the hub caps. The 1975–79 Seville featured the tyres in a way that no Cadillac had done since the late 1920s.

The 1980 Seville was the most sensational new model to be introduced in that year by any manufacturer. It marked a move away from the pursuit of modern form towards the traditional, a move away from the very latest towards the romantic and retrospective.

Station wagons have had simulated timber sides, and Cadillac have borrowed from the aircraft industry for its imagery since 1948, but this was the first time that the imitation of a motoring image from a former era had been so obviously incorporated into a new GM Design. Lincoln had faked the Continental spare wheel into the boot lid of the Mark IV, and Cadillac had imitated the rear fender grilles of the 1950–58 Cadillacs on the 1971–72 Eldorados, but here was a real production Cadillac saying 'Look at me, I am an early fifties English coachbuilt limousine'.

The new model was officially released on the afternoon of Wednesday 26 September 1979, and stole the limelight from the full-sized Cadillacs with its radically different styling. Edward C. Kennard, the Divisions general manager, was quick to put the car into historical context, to find it a statistical niche to identify it for the all-important national papers.

First, he called it the first US car to be sold with a diesel engine as standard, a body combining European flavour and American flair, and the 'first sedan to combine front wheel drive with fully independent four wheel suspension, four wheel disc brakes, electronic levelling control, electronic climate control, and cruise control'.

The name hadn't changed and the front emblems were interchangeable, but technically the new Seville was different in every possible respect. For a start, the rear wheel drive Seville had a unitary body with separate front subframe to support and isolate the front suspension, engine and gearbox. It was Cadillac's first unit construction car, built on the same lines as the other cars that the Seville was aimed at, Rolls-Royce, Mercedes-Benz and Jaguar. The new Seville was built on a separate chassis with the body mounted at 14 points. This frame was identical to the two door Cadillac Eldorado which had been introduced for 1979, it was shared by Oldsmobile's Toronado and Buick's Riviera, even down to the part number. The other three cars had all been built at the GMAD plant at Linden, New Jersey since their introduction for the 1979 model year, and the Seville became the fourth model to be built there.

The Seville had very definitely been rationalized. The measure of the stylist's achievement was that they replaced a model that really was unique, but perhaps didn't look it, with one that was so rationalized that it could be built on the same production line as Eldorados, Toronados and Rivieras. Yet it looked like the most unique car in the industry. The instant description for this radical restyling of the smallest four door Cadillac was 'Hooper Daimler'.

An essential characteristic of this style is the downswept waistline and fully-skirted rear wheels, both features which Cadillac chose to ignore in their reinterpretation of the style developed in the early 1950s by the coachbuilders 'Hooper and Company', who held the royal warrant for coach building from 1830 to 1959, and Freestone and Webb, also of London, who built custom bodies from 1923 to 1957. Hooper designed their bodies

The front end carried over the Seville look from the previous year, presumably for customer continuity

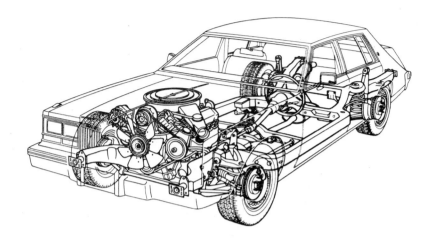

Above *Independent rear suspension and front wheel drive were already features of the previous year's Eldorado, and Oldsmobile Toronado and Buick Riviera from the sister GM divisions. Separate chassis and front torsion bars are evident in this cutaway view*

Right *Deep stainless sill mouldings reduce apparent depth of the sides, with the Elegante script on rear quarter panel*

particularly for Daimler, and Freestone and Webb for Rolls-Royce. The front wing swept right through to the rear bumper, changing from a convex to a concave curve at the front door, the bonnet line bending down with the downswept waistline right through to the back bumper as well. The concave sweep of the rear panel from the back window highlighted the convex curve of the boot lid.

What makes the Hooper design so delightful is the fully skirted rear wheel and the 'S' shaped line of the front wing swept right through to the rear bumper. This gives the car poise in side elevation, and a feeling of movement when standing still. The new Seville did not adopt either of these features.

I asked Bill Mitchell about it all at Claridges Hotel, London, in June 1983 and he was happy to take credit for the concept, one of the last designs he influenced before leaving GM in 1977. 'I used to stay at the Savoy when I came over here by myself, because I liked looking up and down the river and to hear the bells, but my wife prefers this hotel for shopping in Bond Street. Watching the cars coming and circling in the driveway one night I saw the Rolls and Daimler limousines and said to myself if that car was lower it would be good. So we first did a

Mitchell's inspiration, the British Daimler DS420 Limousine. Introduced in 1968 and still current, it is more likely that this is what he saw at the Savoy Hotel than a nineteen-fifties Hooper-bodied Daimler or Rolls-Royce

full sized Cadillac which Cadillac didn't like too much but the time was then closing up for a new Seville so we did this. This time everyone liked it, the conservatives liked it and the extreme men liked it. Now I'm sorry to hear that it's going to be changed in '85 or '86 for something more conservative. I'm not just sorry, it breaks my heart, I love that design.' He drives one himself too.

The actual design of the car was handled by Wayne Kady and his team at the Cadillac studio at GM's Tech Centre at Warren, Michigan, on the other side of Detroit to Cadillac's Clark Avenue.

Wayne Kady has been quoted as saying 'You wanted a unique Cadillac, I have given you a unique Cadillac' from which one might gather that the reaction to the new model was, in the early stages, mixed at least.

Press releases were quick to extol the virtues of the new trunk design, but its increased capacity was really much more due to the space released by the new rear suspension than to any intrinsic merit in the 'bustle' shape. A practical improvement made possible by the removal of the driving axle to the front was that a fully inflated compact spare tyre could now by mounted vestically at the very front of the luggage compartment, out of the way. This is not a good arrangement in the event of actually having a puncture since all the luggage must be lifted out, and the punctured full size wheel is hard to fit into the same space.

Tyres themselves were of a lower profile than previously, size being P205/75 R15.

These tyres were available only in whitewall, with the option of the Uniroyal 'Royal Seal' Anti Puncture tyre, said to be capable of preventing deflation in all but 10 per cent of tread penetrations, providing that the tread area punctured did not exceed 3/16 in. in diameter. 15 × 6 aluminium wheels were standard, with the option on the

Elegante only of a steel wheel with simulated wire wheel cover. Authentic wire wheels for the Seville were now a thing of the past, although they were still available on rear wheel drive Cadillacs.

Heated outside rear mirrors were now standard; these were electrically controlled with an illuminated thermometer to show outside temperatures.

Side window demisting was built into the ventilating system, and the main beams of the headlamps were now tungsten halogen to take advantage of relaxations in federal regulations.

Electrically operated boot closer, optional in 1979, was now standard, and the fibre-optic light monitoring system was continued. Other convenient features carried over from the 1979 model were the illuminated entry system now using a halo lens around the door lock rather than a lens projecting light on to the lock from the door handle above it, illuminated vanity mirrors for both driver and the passenger, and the traditional seat belt chime.

For the more sporting driver, a very effective Sport Handling package was offered comprising

The Seville that never was. Although shown like this in the 1980 brochure, virtually all production Sevilles had Elegante style side-striping sweeping down to the rear bumper; this treatment being considered too severe

harder front and rear springs with 32 mm front anti roll bar and 24 mm rear anti roll bar. Firmer front (though not rear) shock absorbers were also fitted. This package was hardly mentioned in the 1980 brochure, and it would not be until 1982 that the emphasis would start to be put on handling with the introduction of the Eldorado Touring Coupé. This caught the press's imagination with its painted out brightwork and black wall tyres, and stimulated interest in the front wheel drive Cadillacs as cars with sporting pretensions.

Front suspension of the new Seville was by upper and lower A-arms with long torsion bars anchored beneath the front floor. Torsion bars had been introduced with the first of the GM E-body cars, the Oldsmobile Toronado, in 1966 and adopted by the Eldorado in 1967.

Rear suspension was independent using splayed trailing arms with the wheel supported on a stub axle. The medium was a coil spring isolated with an insulator above and below, while the telescopic shock absorber with pneumatic height adjustment was mounted to the rear of the splayed arm, fixed at its top to upward extensions of the main frame. Suspension on the rear wheel drive Seville had been by coils at the front, and a live axle sprung with semi elliptic springs at the back.

The result of all this was that by world standards the Seville had come out of the dark ages by adopting independent rear suspension and simultaneously receded back into them by reverting from a unit construction body to a separate chassis configuration! The Seville had had disc brakes all round since 1977 and these were continued with the new model.

Inside the car there was a considerable improvement in room over the previous model, especially in the back seats. The virtually flat floor gave more leg room, although the engine was still mounted fore and aft, driving the automatic transmission through a chain and sprockets. The increase in space allowed the use of map pockets on the seat back.

On the dashboard the air conditioning controls were moved to render them also accessible to the passenger. There was a new electronic climate control, with LED display and red and blue buttons to raise or lower temperature in one degree increments; and other controls were by push buttons. The radio was mounted below this panel, and the mpg sentinel above it. When the mpg sentinel was not fitted, as with the diesel engine, a Cadillac scripted plate was inserted in this space. 1979 had seen the change over from simulated rosewood to simulated walnut used in combination with simulated chromium to make up the dash panel. Now the 1980 went a stage further by having 'simulated teak woodgrain . . . accented with simulated butterfly walnut inlays'. These inlays actually bordered the four main areas of the dash and were separated by simulated chrome plated metal strips. All this from the same corporation who once owned thousands of acres of their own hardwood forests for automobile body construction.

For the Elegante version a brushed chromium plated metal divider trim swept from above the front sidelamps right through to the rear bumper.

There were three different optional colour combinations and Elegante scripts on the 'C' pillars. 40/40 Dual Comfort seats were fitted as in the rear wheel drive Elegante, with a leather topped console for storage and a single large armrest between the seats. The Elegante strip and dual colours cleverly changed the appearance of the car, making it look rather lower and integrated the front to rear.

The diesel engine that had been an option during 1978 and 1979 became the standard engine for 1980, but 63.2 per cent of buyers opted for gasoline units,

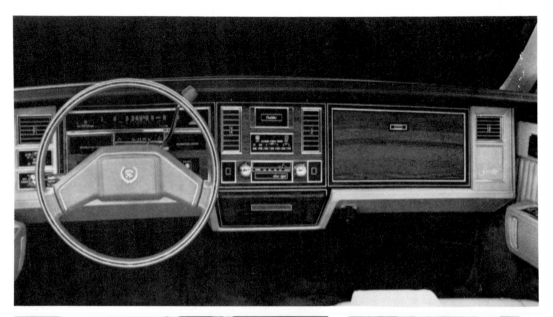

Top *The previous year's information band was replaced by twin information centres more readily seen through the steering wheel, while the air conditioning controls were repositioned so that they could be adjusted by the passenger as well. All metal divider stripes are actually plastic, so is the rosewood and walnut*

Above left *The new style boot held a lot more than the previous model, not least because the fully inflated, space saver spare wheel stood vertically at the front of the compartment*

Above right *The mpg sentinal was available on petrol engines only. The air conditioning controls are all electronic with digital temperature readout*

Roof mounted dual map lights came with storage space for optional garage door opener transmitter

reworked versions of the previous year's 7 litre V8 now reduced to 6 litres, or 360 cu. in., and fitted with digital electronic fuel injection. This system relied more on computer technology than the earlier electronic system and was introduced as part of the continuing compaign for fuel economy. The 5.7 litre continued to be offered as this engine had not been certified for sale in California.

An electronic control module controlled the digital electronic fuel injection, including electronic spark timing and idle speed. Sensors monitored manifold absolute pressure, ambient barometric pressure, engine coolant temperature, incoming mixture temperature, engine speed and throttle position. The idling speed was actually programmed into the computer, being maintained with the car in or out of gear and with the air conditioner on or off. The system also included a diagnostic capability and enabled Cadillac to include an mpg sentinel as standard equipment to compute instant and average mpg.

Unfortunately only two injectors were used, one for each bank of cylinders, and the resulting reduction in power was dramatic, giving 145 bhp as against 180 bhp with the previous 5.7 litre engine, in spite of the increase in capacity. Composite fuel consumption improved to 17 mpg from the previous seasons 16 mph in 1979. The curious anomaly was that the California 350 engine while giving only 160 bhp for 1980 was still devloping 15 bhp more than the 49-state car, when the norm for Californian engines is less power overall.

The average Seville buyer was probably not very interested in all these technicalities, but certainly would have been interested in the appearance of the car and its price. At $19,662 its base price was $4000 up on the 1979, and the buyer of the 1980 had every right to expect a lot of car for his money.

Unfortunately the new Seville did not sell as well as its predecessor. Its first year proved to be its best with 39,344 cars produced as against, for the rear-wheel drive Seville's peak showing—56,985 in 1978.

The recession in the United States coincided with the new Cadillac, and demand was depressed throughout the industry. More than a quarter million auto workers were unemployed so the reduction in sales could be seen as a mark of the excellence of the product.

The engineers had asked for more advanced technology with a modern rear suspension design and front-wheel-drive. Rationalization was achieved by building the car as a variation on the established Eldorado, Toronado and Riviera chassis and drive train, and having it all assembled by GMAD at Linden.

Ford in particular had been copying the international luxury concept and selling it as the Lincoln Versailles, a singularly unattractive design. The GM stylists wanted something so different that Ford wouldn't dare copy it, and Wayne Kady delivered the car he was asked for. As it turned out, both Ford and Chrysler had bustle-trunks for 1982.

The car went on sale, and the marketing people analysed the results. The first surprise was that the new Seville did not appeal to women as much as had the rear wheel drive version. As many as half of the buyers of the early Seville were female, a change Cadillac did not entirely welcome because they did not want the Seville to become a woman's car by association.

The new Seville was not selling, either, to the younger buyer Cadillac wanted to attract. When the first Seville was launched in 1975, it was deliberately youthful, and it was 'international' sized, not smaller. It had combined the roof-line of a Rolls-Royce Silver Shadow, and the wheels of a Jaguar XJ6 with Cadillac glitter; it had made news around the world, even featuring on the covers of enthusiast magazines such as *Car and Driver*. The new Seville looked anything but international and somehow not very youthful, so it was less likely to achieve conquest sales from foreign imports than had been its predecessor.

A successful car company must constantly court youthful buyers—not just keep the existing customers coming back for more. Packard found this out to their cost in the mid-fifties. While most Americans made their last motorized journey on the Cadillac commercial chassis, they were needed as customers very much sooner.

In 1980, it was quite obvious to Cadillac management that the Seville was not the car to open up new markets for Cadillac among younger buyers, but they had their sights, however, firmly set on 1982, when they knew that they would have the 'J' Cimarron and the lively two-door Eldorado Touring Coupé.

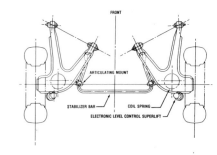

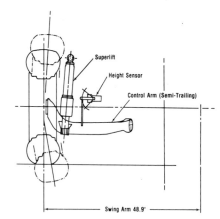

The 1980 Seville independent rear suspension from two view points

The diesels

By 1978, the pressure was on Cadillac to make their cars more economical. For the five years up until the introduction of the Seville in 1975 the 500 cu. in. V8 (8.2 litres) was powering all Cadillacs. This engine, with its excess power capable of giving strong road performance while driving a high output alternator, air pump, power steering pump and air conditioning pump, was hardly giving better than 10 mpg under any circumstances. The corporate average fuel economy legislation was clearly going to force Cadillac to abandon this engine and design one that would be not only more fuel-efficient but lighter as well.

The Seville was one of the smallest and the more expensive Cadillacs in production, so it made sense to introduce diesel power to this model. By introducing the engine as a technical innovation on the top line car, it would then become more acceptable in cheaper larger cars in subsequent years.

The petrol injected 350 was outstandingly economical as compared with any other Cadillac previously offered. On long runs 20 miles per Imperial gallon were really possible, broadening the appeal of the Cadillac marque to drivers who really cared about fuel economy as well as to those who wanted to be fashionably aware of their part in the conservation of natural resources.

The introduction of a diesel was a bold move. Cadillacs are traditionally whisper quiet to the outside observer as well as to the driver and passengers, and all diesels make the traditional knocking noise associated with London taxis or Interstate trucks idling at turnpike toll booths.

Mercedes-Benz had already set a precedent for the use of diesel engines in luxury cars and, as has already been seen, it was potential Mercedes-Benz owners who Cadillac were trying to woo to their Seville. The public image of the Mercedes in the

Manufactured by Oldsmobile, the diesel was an adaption of the existing petrol 350, gave a 50 per cent improvement in fuel economy

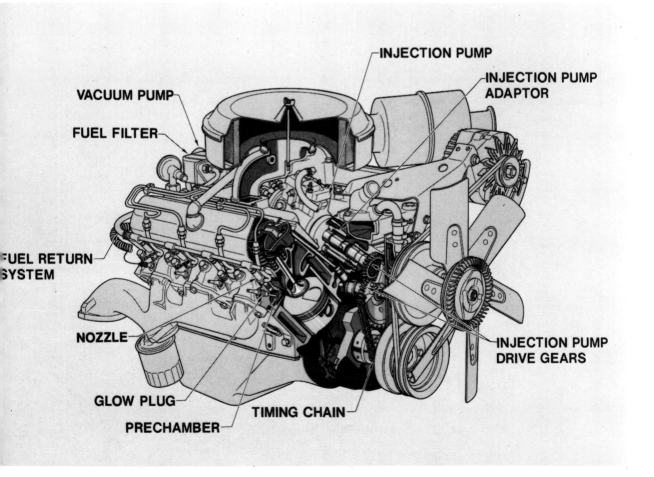

VACUUM PUMP

FUEL FILTER

INJECTION PUMP

INJECTION PUMP ADAPTOR

FUEL RETURN SYSTEM

NOZZLE

INJECTION PUMP DRIVE GEARS

GLOW PLUG

TIMING CHAIN

PRECHAMBER

United States had never been higher, and their association with diesel engines was clearly doing Mercedes no harm at all.

The diesel engined version was launched in the spring of 1978 with a modified compression ignition version of the Oldsmobile 350 which powered all Sevilles. This engine was able to claim a 50 per cent improvement over petrol engined Sevilles according to EPA tests. The city/highway/combined figures were 21/30/24 for the diesel as against 12/19/14 for the L49 petrol engine. For the remainder of the 1978 model run, 1500 diesel engined Sevilles were planned. Unlike the fuel injected L49 engine, which had its final assembly and testing at Cadillac in Detroit, the LF9 diesel was bought in direct from Oldsmobile at Lansing, Michigan. Compression ratio was 22.46 for the diesel as against 7.9 for the gasoline unit, and the SAE net horse power was down to 120 at 3600 rpm from 180 at 4400 rpm.

For 1979, the diesel engine was sold hard, having proved successful in 1978 with a full 5 per cent of the Seville market, in spite of the mid year introduction. The 1979 brochure came with a 'Diesel power for Cadillac' gold embossed booklet listing ten salient features of the diesel engine, including the reasons for the fuel economy advantage and explanations of glow plugs and starting procedures. It emphasized that there was no need for regular tune-ups with no spark plugs, no carburetor or distributor and no conventional ignition system. It also mentioned that oil and filter changes were required at 3000 mile intervals.

In the glove box a directory of 5000 'Diesel Fuel Locations' was provided for the new diesel owner, complete with a warning about restrictions on purchase of diesel fuel in some States. It listed 5000 'green pump' stations in the USA and Canada, from Hayden's Gulf in Alabaster, Alabama to the Porter

Creek Motel in Whitehorse, Yukon.

Dealers were properly primed with diesel sales information as well. The 1979 mechandising guide incorporated a sheet on Diesel Education to assist in the 'enormous task of educating our customers'. It identified two types of people the salesmen might expect to meet, the diesel devotee who needed no persuading, and the other who had only a passing awareness of diesels but was 'almost always approachable in terms of the diesel's benefits'. It also listed five 'Common Objections to Diesel and their Rebuttals'.

More than 10,000 of the 53,487 Sevilles made in 1979 were diesels, and for the great majority of these owners the cars were well up to expectations. They start easily, run smoothly from cold, and the engine does not sound like a diesel once the car is on the move. A considerable reduction in power is of little consequence in everyday motoring. The cruise control works perfectly, and there is no electronic ignition to impose its whine on sensitive after-market stereo systems. At traffic lights the car draws looks of appreciative envy from truckers and cab driver alike.

The fuel economy really is extraordinary. The 21 US gallon tank can give 500 miles between fill-ups. In Europe, where diesel can be up to 50 per cent cheaper than petrol, this is a tremendous advantage, particularly when the latter fuel in these countries costs about three times what it costs in the United States.

For many Europeans, the Seville diesel gives the opportunity to travel in air conditioned Cadillac comfort and silence at fuel cost no higher than that of a small European economy car.

Diesel engines are not fundamentally more economical than petrol units but are very much more frugal with fuel at small and medium throttle openings. Petrol engines run at maximum efficiency

DIESEL SHARE OF TOTAL MERCEDES REGISTRATIONS 1970-1979 CALENDAR YEARS		
	% DIESEL	DIESEL MODELS OFFERED
1970	5.9%	220D
1971	17.6	220D
1972	14.4	220D
1973	14.2	220D
1974	24.9	240D
1975	40.3	240D, 300D
1976	46.5	240D, 300D
1977	46.6	240D, 300D
1978	52.2	240D, 300D 300CD, 300SD
1979 (DELIVERIES)		
JANUARY	65.4	240D, 300D
FEBRUARY	70.2	300CD, 300SD
MARCH	(73.0)	300TD

Mercedes-Benz sales had already proved the existence of the potential market for a Seville diesel

at wide throttle openings, which is why they are so suitable for high performance cars. Diesels are most fuel-efficient at small throttle openings because the speed of the engine is controlled by the amount of fuel injected, and air flow is unimpeded.

In a Cadillac, the unimpeded air flow in the intake manifold means that the vacuum source, which is a useful by-product of the petrol engine, is not available in the diesel. The Cadillac uses vacuum for the power brake servo, for automatic transmission control, to operate the valves and doors in the heating and air conditioning, for the power release of the parking brake, and to power the cruise control diaphragm. For this reason a vacuum pump is fitted at the back of diesel engines where one might expect to see a distributor, to power the last three of these system. The power brakes' master cylinder, the Bendix Hydro Boost, incorporates a hydraulic servo operated by the power steering pump on diesel Cadillacs, and the vacuum operated GM Turbo Hydramatic 400 transmission is replaced by the GM Turbo Hydro 250 which does not use a vacuum control.

The vacuum pump, which provides the power for the car's other systems, is unfortunately notoriously unreliable, and, since it is a sealed unit, it cannot be repaired with just a seal kit.

Driven gently, as suits diesels best, this transmission tends to feel as though it is shifting too late in each gear when accelerating, as would happen were stall speed of the transmission set too high. This is in contrast to the 400, whose vacuum control can arrange upshifts at low revs, and almost imperceptibly, when characteristically Cadillac gentle driving is required.

The hydraulic power brake system has the advantage over the vacuum of being more progressive in operation, adding to the European 'feel' which the Seville strives to achieve.

Driving a diesel Seville is much like driving the petrol version except for a different starting procedure. On turning the ignition, an amber 'wait' lamp glows on the dash strip for up to six seconds, and while there is no switch to prevent cranking of the engine in this position, the glow plugs heat the mixture in the pre-heat chambers until the green

Cadillac's advertising agency Darcy, MacManus & Masius used this advertisement for the new 1978 Seville diesel

'start' lamp comes on. Inevitably this system involves sensors and timers which are prone to failure. General Motors emphasize that starting sprays should not be used with this engine in particular, so failure of the glow plug starting system can leave the owner in a difficult position. It must be said that starting fluids will start this diesel without the glow plugs being operational, but in the light of the warnings on top of the air cleaner pan it is as well to reserve this method for emergencies only.

The Wait and Start lamps on the drivers indicator strip are substituted for the red and green economy lamps on the petrol-engined version, and are just as hard to read without the help of a shading hand on sunny days!

Anyone who drives a GM diesel engined car built in the 1970s will have heard the dire warnings from enthusiasts and mechanics alike about the inherent weaknesses of the engine.

Before considering the problems which have occurred it is worth remembering that the owner has certain responsibilities which must be observed.

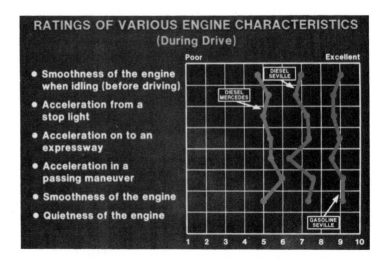

Car Clinic evaluations of the Mercedes against the 350 Seville petrol and diesel

The first of these is regular oil changing at recommended 3000 mile intervals. By modern standards this is pathetically short, but most engine failures are due to this particular rule's being ignored. A diesel engine with its inherently less refined fuel pollutes engine oil faster. At the same time it makes greater demands on the strength of the oil because of its much higher compression ratio. A diesel engine also gives full power from cold, thereby permitting an unsympathetic driver to subject the engine bearings to high stress before the oil has reached its working temperature.

American drivers are notorious for forgetting basic servicing and oil changes. The author has driven in the USA a 95,000 mile Thunderbird which had definitely never had an oil or filter change since the car was built, although the oil level had been topped up occasionally! Seville diesels that are neglected like this break their crankshafts.

Unfortunately for Oldsmobile, who build this engine and must carry some of the blame for its problems, popular myths about diesels die hard. Encouraged by the introductory advertising that emphasized the end of spark plug changes and carburettor tuneups, the new driver didn't bother to get his car serviced. He'd seen those 18-wheel rigs pass him on the freeway at 75mph, looking so powerful that they could never stop for anything so mundane as an oil change. Who could blame him for thinking that he, like the trucker, could not drive for ever with his toe to the board, showing just a sooty tail pipe to his brethren in otherwise similar cars who had not discovered the sweet and frugal mythology of diesel power.

What he didn't know was that diesel trucks have multiple gearboxes to enable them to run these speeds at very low revs. They also use special lubricating oils which are not compatible with the Olds/Cadillac 350 engine based on a conventional

'79 Seville diesel rear emblem. Cadillac didn't try to hide the fact

gasoline unit, and most have governors to restrict their engine speed. Cadillac emphasized the importance of oil changes on the driver's sun visor and in other literature, but 3000 miles represent a very short interval between oil changes; a diesel owner in New York who had his car serviced before taking a return trip to Los Angeles would need his oil and filter changed before he was back into Arizona.

Apart from a tendency on the injection piping and return system to leak and for the rather expensive injector pumps to fail prematurely the big problem on the early diesel engines, before engine serial number 152880 was stretching cylinder head bolts. Previously, these had been the same bolts as used on the EFI engines which had only a third of the compression and these had been found to stretch in service. To remedy this problem, five new high tensile bolt designs were introduced into the cylinder head. All these bolts are marked with a special identification bar or yellow dye on the head surface.

General Motors were quick to react to continuing problems associated with the diesel, and continued to improve the engine and its ancillaries. For owners in trouble, they were generous in their policy of 'adjustment'. In 1981 the service interval on the 350 diesel was improved to 5000 from the previous 3000 miles, thanks to the introduction of roller type camshaft followers. In 1983 a bargain-priced 'Target-master' engine became available, incorporating all the latest changes, fully equipped and ready to run, for the owners of older diesel powered cars whose engines wanted replacement.

In 1983 model year only 670 diesel Sevilles were produced, a volume that must be making Cadillac wonder whether they now need to offer such a version at all.

Detroit, Linden and Tehran

Production of the new Seville started on 26 March 1975 in the old Eldorado assembly building at Cadillac's Clark Avenue complex in Detroit, which had been built between 1920 and 1927 on what is now a fairly restricted site.

Cadillac had not previously built a unitary body car, and this presented certain problems. Hence the build rate was only 14 cars per hour during early production.

The unit body of the Seville was delivered by the Fisher Body Division with everything forward of the bulkhead detached. This was because the turning radii at the Cadillac plant did not permit handling of the full body on the old line. The Seville had been designed with bolt-on front panels and separate subframe partly for this reason.

Production of the car was computer-controlled so that components arrived to the correct specification and colour at each work station. A new pedestal conveyor was introduced which carried the chassis to eight working stations, past the body drop operation for consistent front end sheet metal fit. The Seville was one of the first cars to make extensive use of Zincrometal, a type of steel coated with zinc-rich primer before forming; bi-metal anti-corrosion systems were also used in manufacture. Many of the sheet metal components came from Cadillac's Conner Avenue plant in Detroit, and were also finished and painted at the Clark Avenue plant.

1977 production at Clark Avenue. Here, a painted body, with rear subframe already built in, is dropped onto the rear axle and springs and engine subframe assembly

Installation of front end components in 1977. Who's trapped his fingers?

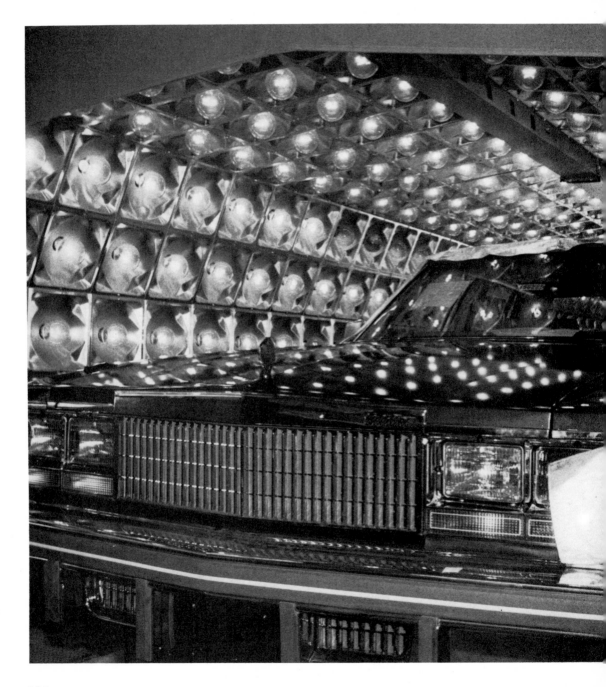

Left *Not testing to see if it really glitters but just giving it a final bake, after repairs to the paintwork following assembly*

Above *Preparation for shipping, the screen sticker says 'export'*

The Cadillac/Buick/Chevrolet assembly plant at Tehran

The 350 cu. in. engine, brought in from Oldsmobile, was checked cold before being fitted with its fuel injection and ignition systems and was then test-run on petrol before installation into the car. Cylinder heads were modified by Cadillac to take the fuel injectors. More than 200,000 cars were built at the West assembly plant before rear wheel drive production finished in 1979 the building reverting to storage and sub-assemblies.

By the end of the 1976 model year 60,000 Sevilles had been built and many had been exported to Europe and the Middle East. The car was just as popular as had been predicted for Europe, offering a comparable ride and level of silence to a Rolls-Royce, as well as better fuel economy and a great advantage over the standard size Cadillac in that it could be parked in a normal meter space. In England, the distributors organized a right-hand-

Breaking open crates of Seville parts in Tehran

drive conversion by Wooler Hodack and in the rest of Europe, particularly in Belgium, Germany and Holland, the car was very popular in its left-hand-drive form.

The escalation of oil prices which was killing GM's traditional market for big-engined cars, was making the middle eastern oil countries rich, and leaving them with money to invest in industrial projects. The stablest of these countries was Iran. It had a royal family respected throughout the world, and the Shah was a friend of western leaders, a regular visitor to Europe and the United States. The US kept a military presence in Iran, and the oil industry was mainly under European or American control. GM decided to assemble Sevilles in Tehran.

This was one of the shortest-lived of GM's assembly plants. It is easy to be wise in retrospect, but to GM management in 1976, when the plant

The body assembly area in Tehran, and then their body drop section

Below *Finished Iranian cars, these were all fitted with a non-emission, special high output engine which gave at least 20 bhp more than the domestic car*

Aerial view of Linden, New Jersey. Producing Sevilles from 1980 onwards together with Eldorados, Buick Rivieras and Oldsmobile Toronados, it is one of General Motors most profitable operations

must have been planned, none of the Middle Eastern countries looked more suitable for such a venture.

Six Cadillac employees and their families went to Iran in mid January, 1977. These employees collectively represented, manufacturing, engineering, service, reliability and quality assurance disciplines that were needed to develop the facilities and begin car production.

The assembly plant complex in Tehran was set up to produce not only Sevilles but also Chevrolet Nova and Buick Skyhawk models, all operations housed in one building; Chevrolet trucks were handled in a second building. A third building contained assembly facilities for Jeep and Jeep Wagoneer models as part of a joint venture programme with the local AMC distributors. The chassis assembly operations for the Seville and the Chevrolet-Buick models were combined but the Seville body assembly line was entirely separate. The operation was set up to assemble CKD (completely knocked down) kits with almost all body chassis and engine components shipped in from Canada where their components were crated.

The first Iranian Seville was finished on 1 March 1977, being hand-built on the unfinished assembly line. Production proper started in June with the first 70–80 cars finished in gold to commemorate an Iranian event. All these cars went to the Iranian government for use by government officials or military personnel.

President Carter visited Iran in December 1977 and the political troubles started in January 1978, the same month that Cadillac's manufacturing representative left, his job completed. Most of the other Cadillac employees had returned to the US during the previous summer.

Against an increasingly difficult political background, culminating in the national strikes in September, approximately 800–1000 Sevilles were assembled by local labour before operations had to cease.

On 1 February 1979 the Ayatollah Kohmeni arrived at Tehran airport from Paris. His jubilant

Iranian Sevilles had second script on left side of boot lid; it reads Cadillac, and then another word which could be 'injection' but is not readily identifiable from this photograph

111

followers were headed by his holy vehicle, another GM product, a Chevrolet Blazer.

2100 CKD kits had been sent out from Canada and less than 1000 were assembled, so it is clear that approximately 1000 unassembled Sevilles were either destroyed or may still exist. Each crate contained quantities of only one part, so that anyone wanting to build up even one Seville would have to find all the boxes!

General Motors of Iran became Pars Khodro after the revolution, and an enquiry to them in August 1983 brought the reply that only 37 Sevilles had been assembled since the revolution, and that nothing was known of the missing CKD kits. Perhaps only General Motors could apparently lose more than one million dollars worth of cars and not make at least a well publicized fuss about it! At present this must remain one of motoring's unsolved mysteries. Chrysler Corporation still maintains a presence in Iran through its English subsidiary, which sends out CKD Hillman Hunters from Coventry, and had been doing so for years.

Seville went front wheel drive in 1980, and was built on the same chassis of the two-door Eldorado as well as the Riviera and Toronado. These were already being assembled at the General Motors Assembly Division plant at Linden, New Jersey, and it was partly the rationalization of production to this plant which enabled the new Seville to be such a technically sophisticated car. The Seville and Eldorado operation is one of General Motors' most profitable enterprises ever.

Cadillac management were certainly sorry to lose production of their most expensive car to another division, and dispute the Corporate view that GMAD are the experts both in car assembly and effective quality control. All four models are produced on the same production line, the bodies arriving from Fisher.

Maturity

For 1981 the diesel was again offered as a standard engine for the Seville, an option taken up by only a quarter of all buyers. All diesels now had a water-in-fuel detection system to alert the driver to a condition that will stop any diesel in its tracks. The reduced popularity of the diesel was due to a levelling of prices between the two fuels, renewed stabilization of petrol supplies, and economy improvements in petrol engines.

The six litre engine was modified to run on 4, 6 or 8 cylinders as determined by the onboard digital computer in the digital fuel injection system. This unit was known as the V8-6-4, and used an electro-mechanical device to simultaneously deactivate both the inlet and exhaust valves of the cylinder by moving the fulcrum point of the rocker arm. The theory is good, and this was another Cadillac first—but in practice the fuel savings achieved by this engine were disappointing, and the V8-6-4 was destined to be dropped by Cadillac after only one year of service, except for limousines where its power output continued to be useful for such heavy cars. Unfortunately, this multi-displacement engine was also unreliable and suffered intermittent computer faults early in 1981, leaving the owner with a car which did not fail safe on to, say, four cylinders but stopped completely.

The other optional petrol engine was Buick's carburetted V6. This was the first V6 to be offered in a Seville and the first without injection. This V6 of

The 1981 had a Seville script ahead of the front wheel. This is an Elegante shown with optional simulated wire wheels

4.1 litres capacity had been introduced by Buick as their top line engine for the 1980 model year. It was still 20 bhp more powerful than the faithful 5.7 diesel and delivered more torque. There were also recognizable external differences between the 1980 and 1981 cars, the most obvious being that the Seville badge on the side of the car was moved from behind the front wheel to a position ahead of it, and just behind the front cornering lamp. An air dam was now fitted below the front bumper, and the tail lamps came with new winged crests, reminiscent of Cadillac's 1941 style. The wreath and crest on both the aluminium wheels and the optional wire wheel covers was now gold, and the Elegante brushed moulding became standard on all Sevilles. The Elgante could still be distinguished externally by its script, dual colour combinations now being available on the standard car. 1981 was the best selling year for the Elegante, one Seville in five being the luxury model.

German registered 'variable displacement' 1981 in Luxembourg

A brand new Cadillac V8 engine of 4.1 litres led the line-up for 1982, being available on all models except the limousines and the new four-cylinder J-bodied Cimarron. This new engine was the first all-new General Motors V8 in fifteen years, and was designed with light weight and fuel efficiency in mind. The engine block was of die cast aluminium, with free-standing cast iron cylinders and separate die cast aluminium valve lifter carrier. Cylinder heads were cast iron and the inlet manifold of aluminium. The water pump was also of aluminium, and the engine was 209 lb lighter than the previous six litre V8. It came with a 4-speed automatic.

Throttle body injection was used again with an electronic control module to compute electronic spark timing, mixture and constant idle speed. Belt tightening was by jack-screws rather than by slotted brackets and other accessories were care-

The new 'bustle' Seville was not the success in Europe that its predecessor had been

Above *The 1981 Seville, now with Elegante-type mouldings*

Left *Apart from its engine identification badge, the 1982 Seville can only be told from the '81 by its black rather than grey bumper inserts. This is a diesel, with simulated wire covers and self sealing anti-puncture tyres*

119

The 1983 Seville has fine meshed radiator grille with thinner top moulding and 'Cadillac' script moved down to grille

fully integrated including an auxiliary vacuum pump and a power steering pump with remote fluid reservoir.

Manufactured at Cadillac's own fully automated Livonia, Michigan plant, this was now the standard engine for the Seville. The diesel became an option and accounted for only 11.9 per cent of sales. The V6 was also offered. With the base price now at $23,433, perhaps it was not surprising that total production was only 20,000 cars.

In 1983 the price of the Seville was slashed by

almost $2000 and, helped perhaps by some changes to the front of the car which made it obvious who had the new ones, sales increased and soared production to 30,430. The V6 engine was dropped, so once again all Sevilles were fuel-injected; only a tiny 2.2 per cent were diesels.

The new grille had less vertical emphasis, and five, rather than two, intermediate horizontal bars and a shallower moulding immediately above it on the bonnet. The Cadillac script was moved down on to the grille, and as a subtle touch reminiscent of the

1983 model rear view with 'Touring Suspension' emblem at left of the boot lid

Top *1983 air conditioning controls had electronic outside temperature indication from a sensor mounted behind the grille, temperature could be indicated in fahrenheit or centigrade*

Above *When ordered with the optional digital instrument panel, readout could be either in metric or imperial units. Note also the four speeds on the automatic transmission indicator*

very first Sevilles, front parking lenses were now clear again.

To render the lower base price viable, a number of previously standard features were put on the 'available' list. These included the heated outside mirrors, internal illuminated vanity mirrors, the twilight sentinel and even the tilt and telescopic steering wheel. Wire wheel covers now became optional, replaced by a plain pressed cover, and aluminium wheels also became an extra cost option. For 1983 these were of a truly sporting design with 36 radial slots and exposed chromium lug nuts. The sports handling package was renamed the Touring Suspension, and now included larger, low-profile P225/70 R15 steel radials, and the power steering valving was changed to give greater effort and feedback; it is very effective.

The chime tones for the seat belt, key left in ignition and headlamps left on modes now each had their own particular tone. It started to become clear by 1983 that the radically styled 'bustle trunk' Seville was now becoming accepted, and it had quite noticeably become one of the favourite cars of the older but active and affluent age group who winter in Palm Beach or San Diego and are seen at White Sulphur Springs or Lake Tahoe in the summer. Median age of Seville buyers is 58.

Introduced mid-year in 1982, for those who like to be seen in a convertible but wouldn't like to feel any draught, a full cabriolet roof treatment was offered again for 1983 (it was in fact a mid-year introduction in 1982) which simulated the appearance of a true convertible roof complete with canvas-style fabric in a choice of four colours. It is a treatment that suits the Seville remarkably well, giving a new emphasis to the shape of the tail. The canvas convertible top is imitated in every detail including padding over roof bows and the top rear seam cover strip, and slightly uneven seams around the edges.

By the end of the 1983 model year 3736 Cabriolet Sevilles had been sold.

For the penultimate year of the series, the 1984 Seville has lost its engine identification emblem behind the front wheel. It now features a side moulding in body colour and a winged emblem on the parking lamp lenses, and clear outer rear lenses.

Not all the interiors were leather. This 1984 model shows thick velour 'button back'

SEVILLE INTERIOR

Undeniable beauty. Undeniable comfort. Your first glance, your first touch will confirm it. This is first class. From the classic spaciousness to the contemporary color and texture. In 1984 there's a new tufted multi-buttoned seat trim design. It's shown here in the standard Heather knit cloth in Dark Blue, one of four colors offered. Or you may choose the available leather seating areas in any of ten colors.

Even with the extra year and half of production still to come, it now seems unlikely the total of front-wheel-drive deliveries will match the rear-drive Seville's 215,000; but if each of these cars made on American soil represents a Mercedes-Benz or a Jaguar that hasn't been sold, then Cadillac have more than fulfilled their original goal.

1984 with a full cabriolet roof, complete with impression of the hood frame and uneven seam above the side windows

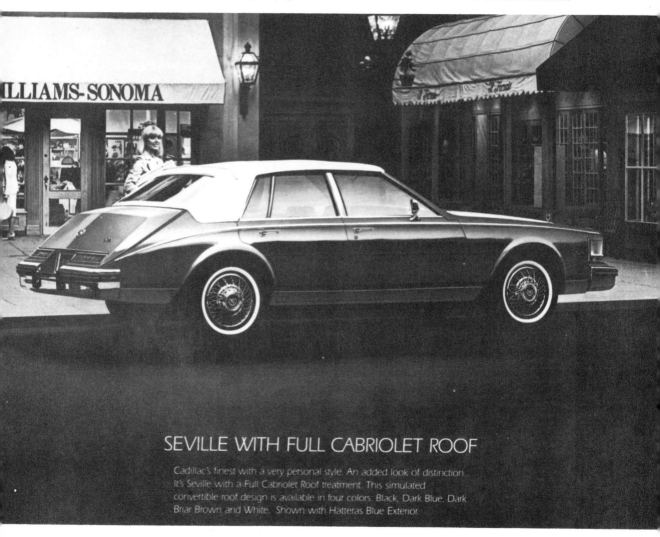

SEVILLE WITH FULL CABRIOLET ROOF

Cadillac's finest with a very personal style. An added look of distinction. It's Seville with a Full Cabriolet Roof treatment. This simulated convertible roof design is available in four colors: Black, Dark Blue, Dark Briar Brown and White. Shown with Hatteras Blue Exterior.

What's really happened—the Seville has lost its 'European' edge on the market, and became more limousine like than ever. Make the comparisons

Notes on American model years

Whilst in Europe we accept the date of first registration as the nominal manufacture date of the car, a system emphasized in Great Britain since 1963 by the use of suffix and now prefix letters for the registration number, American cars are always identified by their year of manufacture or *model year*.

The system started because American manufacturers have traditionally face-lifted their cars every year and any year of an American car, be it a Seville, Thunderbird or Chrysler, will have specific characteristics relating only to that year. A number or letter in the vehicle identification number (the VIN) identifies it as that year, and this plate is normally displayed on the left hand windscreen pillar or near it on top of the dash.

The model year is three months out of phase with the calendar year. For example a 1979 Seville, the last with rear wheel drive and the old body shape and the first with convex right-hand mirror-glass and 'twenty to four' steering wheel might have been manufactured any time from the beginning of September 1978 when the assembly plant reopened after retooling to mid-summer 1979 when it would have closed for the annual holiday of assembly line workers and the retooling. Since demand is usually at its highest with the announcement of face-lifted models at the beginning of the new model year, approximately one third of the 1979 models will have actually been made during calendar year 1978.

Seville year identification

Any year of Seville can be identified at a glance without referring to its VIN number by the following *most significant* changes to basically equipped cars. For detail differences see the forgoing text.

1975–76	new body style, egg-crate grille, 3-spoke wheel
1977	radiator grille extended through to bonnet, new fine mesh grille, 2-spoke steering wheel
1978	overriders on rear bumper, body colour lower side bump strip
1979	convex glass to righthand external mirror, new steering wheel
1980	new body style, script behind front wheel
1981	Seville script moved ahead of front wheel
1982	HT-4100 emblem, grey bumper insert mouldings (1981 and 1983 black)
1983	Horizontal emphasis front grille with reduced top moulding
1984	No engine identification badge, new emblem for front parking lights, new glass for rear lights

A 1979 Seville would typically have a VIN number 6S69N99497769. The sixth digit, being a 9 denotes the model year 1979. Other years below:

Year	VIN
1975–76	. . . . . 6 . . . .
1977	. . . . . 7 . . . . . .
1978	. . . . . 8 . . . .
1979	. . . . 9 . . . .
1980	. . . . . A . . . .
1981	. . . . B . . . . . .
1982	. . . . C . . . . . .
1983	. . . . D . . . . . .
1984	. . . . E . . . . . .

The rest of the VIN is built up as follows.

1	'6'	=Cadillac Division
2	'S'	=Seville
3, 4	'69'	=4 door sedan
5	'N'	=5.7 litre diesel, 'B' would be 5.7 litre EFI
6	'9'	=model year (197<u>9</u>)
7	'9'	=plant code (Cadillac, Detroit)
8–13	'497769'	=serial number

VIN numbers went to 17 characters in 1981. A 1984 Seville would typically have the number

1G6A S6989E E803946.

1	'1'	=USA
2	'G'	=General Motors
3	'6'	=Cadillac
4	'A'	=manual seat belts
5	'S'	=Seville
6, 7	'69'	=4 door sedan
8	'8'	=4.1 V8
9	'9'	=check digit
10	'E'	=model year, i.e. 1984
11	'E'	=plant code, Linden, New Jersey
12–17	'803946'	=serial number

Specifications

Engines

Engine	Type	Comp. ratio	Available	SAE bhp @rpm
5.7 litre EF1	V-8	8.0:1	75–79	180@4400
			80	California only
5.7 litre diesel	V-8	22.5:1	mid 78–84	105@3200
6.0 litre DFI	V-8	8.2:1	80	145@3600
6.0 litre DFI V8–6–4	V-8	8.2:1	81	140@3800
4.1 litre carb.	V-6	8.0:1	81–82	125@3800
4.1 litre DFI	V-8	8.5:1	82–84	125@4200

Engine	SAE torque @rpm ft/lb	Bore x stroke (in.)
5.7 litre EFI	275@2000	4.057×3.385
5.7 litre diesel	205@1600	4.057×3.385
6.0 litre DFI	270@2000	3.800×4.060
6.0 litre DFI V8–6–4	265@1400	3.800×4.060
4.1 litre carb.	210@2000	3.965×3.400
4.1 litre DFI	200@2200	3.465×3.307

Chassis

	Wheelbase in.	Height in.	Length in.	Width in.	Fuel US Gal	Tyre size radial ply
1975–79	114.3	54.7	204.0	71.8	21.0	GR 78–15B
1980–84	114.0	54.3	204.8	70.9	20.3–22.8	P205/75R15

	Track front	rear	Kerb weight typical lb	Steering ratio variable type	Std axle
1975–79	61.3	59.0	4179–4406	16.4:1–13.8:1	2.56:1 3.08 option
1980–84	59.3	60.6	3814–4185	15:1–13:1	2.41 (80–81) 3.15 (82–84)

Seville historical data

	1975	1976	1977	1978	1979
Domestic US deliveries/sales	15,949	41,662	41,135	54,148	45,886
Production (incl. Canada & export)	16,355	43,772	45,060	56,985	53,487
Diesel per cent	N/A	N/A	N/A	5.0	20.1
Base price**$ (at model introduction time)	12,479	12,479	13,359	14,267	15,646

	1980	1981	1982	1983
Domestic US deliveries/sales	39,480	26,622	22,334	30,000
Production (incl. Canada & export)	39,344	28,631	19,998	30,430
Diesel per cent	36.8*	25.4*	11.9	2.2
Base price**$ (at model introduction time)	19,662	21,088	23,433	21,440

*The 5.71 V8 diesel was the standard engine in the Seville for 1980 and 1981. The 6.01 V8 *in 1980* and the 6.01 V8–6–4 *in 1981* were the optional petrol engines offered for those respective years at no additional cost to the customer

**Base price changes reflect economic increases as well as content (equipment/feature) additions (or deletions such as for 1983) to the base car

Bibliography

One book stands out head and shoulders above anything else in my Cadillac library and that is *Cadillac the Complete History* by New Zealander Maurice D. Hendry published by Automobile Quarterly, 3rd Edition 1979.

I have also consulted in preparation of this book *Cadillac Standard of Excellence* by the Editors of Consumer Guide, Castle Books 1980.

Classic Cars Cadillac by Le Roi Smith and Tony Hossain, Colour Library Books Ltd, 1983.

The Encyclopaedia of the American Automobile, Carl Ludvigsen and David Burgess Wise, Orbis Publishing, 1982.

Annual brochures and Cadillac Merchandising Guides published by Cadillac Motor Car Division.

Cadillac Parts and Illustration catalogues published by General Motors Parts Division.

Parts and Accessories Numerical Price List published by General Motors Warehousing and Distribution Division.

Cadillac Seville Attracts World News Spotlight, July 1975, *The American Answer*, October 1975.

'Annual News From Cadillac' press releases, all supplied by Cadillac Public Relations Department.

Acknowledgements

The author particularly thanks the following for their help; Gordon Horsburgh and Charles Gibson at Cadillac and Bill Mitchell for finding time to be interviewed in London.

Thanks also must go to Carl Lawrence; Cadillac Public Relations office; GMAD Public Relations; Lendrum and Hartman in Hammersmith, London; Ken Jestes in Baltimore; the Kirks family in Washington DC; Braman Cadillac in Miami, Florida; Capitol Cadillac in Washington DC; Frankel Cadillac in Baltimore and Chrisman Cadillac in Birmingham, Michigan. The best photographs used here are by GM Photographic, from Cadillac's own archives. Other photographs came from Carl Lawrence, Jerry Sloniger, Tim Parker, Gerald Foster and even the author's own lens.

Frankly we are lucky to have any photographs at all. The sum total of original photographs, colour included, were lost in transit in the UK via the rail network's secure service. All had to be replaced in ten days to meet the printer's deadline—and that included a rescue mission flight to Detroit by the author.

Index

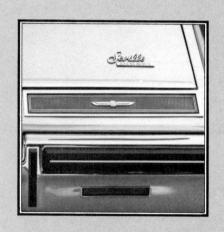

NICK DIGIOVANNI
KNIFE DROP

NICK DIGIOVANNI
KNIFE DROP
CREATIVE RECIPES ANYONE CAN COOK

PHOTOGRAPHY BY MAX MILLA

Publisher Mike Sanders
Senior Editor Ann Barton
Editor Christopher Stolle
Art & Design Director William Thomas
Assistant Director of Art & Design Rebecca Batchelor
Photographer Max Milla
Food Stylist Judean Sakimoto
Recipe Testers Ashley Brooks, Manya Lulek
Proofreaders Megan Douglass, Claire Safran
Indexer Johnna VanHoose Dinse

First American Edition, 2023
Published in the United States by DK Publishing
1745 Broadway, 20th Floor, New York, NY 10019

Published in the United States by Dorling Kindersley Limited

Library of Congress Catalog Number: 2022950019
ISBN 978-0-7440-7677-6

DK books are available at special discounts when purchased in
bulk for sales promotions, premiums, fundraising, or
educational use. For details, contact: SpecialSales@dk.com.

Printed and bound in China

Photographs © 2023 by Max Milla, with the exception of the
following: page 9 © Matt Frost/FOX; page 11, author (family
photographs); pages 17, 18 © Cheryl Clegg

For the curious
www.dk.com

FOR MY **FAMILY, FRIENDS, AND FANS**

CONTENTS

FOREWORD

When Nick first stepped into the MasterChef kitchen, I could immediately sense his talent. From the first dish he prepared to secure his place on the show–a Persian-inspired lamb and mint raviolo–to his brilliant finale appearance, it was evident that he was definitely going places. Even though he didn't win, I knew I had to keep my eyes on him.

Fast forward to now, and Nick has taken the passion I saw in that competition and applied it to the digital food world.

Nick has become the go-to person when it comes to recipes on social media. His creations are fun, original, and accessible to a new generation of savvy home cooks. And, just like on social media, the recipes in this book reflect his culinary journey not just from the MasterChef kitchen but the several kitchens he's trained in, ranging from top-ranked seafood spots to Michelin three-star restaurants. All of this is visible on the pages. Whether it's the Smoky Mezcal Rigatoni or the Persian Street Corn, he's showcasing both his kitchen background and the fun that you can have in the kitchen. As a native New Englander, Nick is also fortunate to have access to some of the best seafood anywhere in the world— as is clear from his seafood dishes such as the Browned Butter Lobster Roll or Shrimp Ceviche.

Just as he does on YouTube, Instagram, and TikTok, Nick breathes fresh energy into cooking and makes it accessible to chefs of all ages—young, old, and everyone in between. That's why I'm so excited for you to start cooking with these recipes. I promise if you cook something from this cookbook, it will receive nothing but praise from me!

Enjoy!

Gordon x

INTRODUCTION

This isn't my first cookbook. I wrote one at seven years old, but nobody bought it. Perhaps because there was only one copy; at least that's what I've told myself. While I don't quite remember all of the recipes inside that green binder, I like to think they reflected the same passion and beliefs I have about food today. Namely, that anyone can cook. Whether I knew it or not at the time, that's what I believed then, and that's what I believe now.

As a kid, while most students filled their lunch boxes with fruit snacks or chips, I brought raw, crushed-up ramen noodles with the seasoning packets poured over them. My favorite was the creamy chicken flavor. Instead of a typical lemonade stand, I recruited my three younger brothers as sous chefs and servers for a small food stand at the bottom of our driveway. We served playful, creative fare, such as hand-churned vanilla ice cream with homemade blueberry coulis—yes, I used the word "coulis" at our neighborhood food stand. Not to worry, we still had classic, artisan lemonade too. We also threw occasional fine-dining dinners for my parents, until we lit the entire grill on fire one evening.

Almost two decades later, I am proud and humbled to be sharing a book that I hope will inspire many people. When it comes to cooking, it doesn't matter if you're young and just beginning to experiment in the kitchen or older and well seasoned. *Anyone can cook.* But what, exactly, makes a *great* cook? I have friends who consider tossing a frozen pizza in the oven "cooking."

No. Please, no.

Before I discuss what it means to cook, why should you listen to me? I have dedicated my *entire* life to learning about food. I've worked 15-hour days in a Michelin three-star kitchen.

Created the first-ever undergraduate food degree at Harvard. Wrote my college thesis advised by Michael Pollan, one of the world's most influential food writers. I've soaked up techniques from several generations of my multiethnic family. Even learned from Gordon Ramsay himself. And I still wake up hungry, each and every day, to learn more. *Knife Drop* is a result of all these years of learning and experimentation. It's a compilation of everything I've learned, infused into 100 recipes containing practical tips and tricks.

So what makes a good cook? Fearlessness. The best food comes from fearlessness. While a good cook knows the best practices, a great cook actively looks for ways to bend and break those very rules. This book will help you master the best practices, and then hopefully give you enough confidence to break them yourself. This will lead to new flavors and culinary experiences that I promise will awaken your taste buds.

As the late Anthony Bourdain said, "There is a real danger of taking food too seriously." Sure, there are some strict, traditional French techniques that are unavoidable when it comes to cooking. But food and cooking, above all else, should be enjoyable. Cooking is the purest form of art, and the only one that involves all five senses. You can and should utilize these senses in any way you'd like. You should use cooking to make *you* happy. Don't let rules get in the way.

Which leads me to this. You've probably never heard the *full* version of the famous quote from the movie *Ratatouille*: "Anyone can cook . . . but only the fearless can be great."

Forget the rules. Just cook!

Cooking

Nicholas Channing DiGiovanni

KITCHEN BASICS

EVEN THE BEST CHEF WILL STRUGGLE WITHOUT PROPER EQUIPMENT.

MUST-HAVE EQUIPMENT

8-INCH CHEF'S KNIFE

KNIFE SHARPENER

BENCH SCRAPER

WOOD CUTTING BOARD

SMALL DISHWASHER-SAFE CUTTING BOARD

NESTING GLASS MIXING BOWLS

CAST-IRON SKILLET

STAINLESS STEEL SKILLET

LARGE NONSTICK SKILLET

LARGE DUTCH OVEN OR HEAVY-BOTTOMED POT

RIMMED BAKING SHEETS

WIRE COOLING RACK

SILICONE NONSTICK BAKING MAT

PRE-CUT PARCHMENT PAPER

MEASURING CUPS (DRY AND LIQUID)

MEASURING SPOONS

METAL WHISK

METAL SPATULA

METAL TONGS

RUBBER SPATULA

SILICONE PASTRY BRUSH

POTATO RICER OR FOOD MILL

FINE-MESH STRAINER OR CHINOIS

BOX GRATER

MICROPLANE GRATER

VEGETABLE PEELER

INSTANT-READ THERMOMETER

ROLLING PIN

FOOD PROCESSOR

HIGH-SPEED BLENDER

HAND MIXER OR STAND MIXER

MUST-HAVE INGREDIENTS

HIGH-HEAT COOKING OIL
For deep frying or pan frying, choose a neutral-tasting, refined oil with a high smoke point. I recommend a good, flavorless vegetable oil, though peanut oil, corn oil, refined avocado oil, or several others work just as well.

OLIVE OIL
Choose a high-quality, extra-virgin olive oil and store it in a cool, dark environment. A good olive oil can be used both for cooking (low to medium heat) and finishing.

BUTTER
For cooking, I prefer unsalted, high-quality butter such as Kerrygold. If I'm using butter to finish a dish or for toast, I'll opt for salted. Always refrigerate butter in an airtight container; otherwise, it will take on flavors and odors from your fridge.

CLARIFIED BUTTER
If you're looking for that classic butter flavor but are cooking at higher temperatures, use clarified butter. It's butter without the milk solids that burn easily. It's a much better option for pancakes, for instance.

SALT
When it comes to salt, have one multipurpose kosher salt purchased in bulk, and one textured salt for finishing, such as flaky sea salt.

SEASONINGS
Buy a few high-quality spices based on your personal taste preferences. My favorites are smoked paprika, fresh peppercorns, ground sumac, garlic powder, onion powder, and seasoned or flavored salts. Some spices, such as pepper and nutmeg, should be freshly ground at the last minute.

PANTRY STAPLES
Invest in high-quality pantry staples, especially those that last a while, such as soy sauce, honey, tomato sauce, mayonnaise, ketchup, maple syrup, mustard, salsa, and dressings. They may cost a few dollars more, but they're worth the investment.

FRESH CITRUS
I love using lemon, lime, and orange zest to brighten up dishes. Make sure, however, that you're using organic or pesticide-free citrus fruits for those you're going to zest.

FRESH HERBS
Because of my Persian background, fresh herbs and spices are a must for me. There is simply no substitute for fresh herbs: dill, mint, basil, cilantro, parsley—you name it. Store herbs refrigerated, wrapped in damp paper towels and in a sealed plastic bag.

CHEESE
Always grate your own cheese. Pre-shredded cheese often contains added chemicals and preservatives. Freshly grated cheese is tastier, more cost-effective, and even melts better.

ROTISSERIE CHICKEN
It's delicious, versatile, and a total bargain. A humble rotisserie chicken is better than nearly any chicken dish you can order at a restaurant.

FEARLESSNESS
While this so-called "ingredient" can't quite be measured, it's the most important one in my pantry. Command your kitchen!

TIPS + TRICKS

Master techniques, not recipes.

Don't open the oven or grill for extended periods of time. Open it quickly, do what you need to do, and close it right up! Move quickly, and with purpose.

Don't blindly follow any recipes—even mine. Everything from oven type to altitude impacts the way food is cooked. Trust your instincts above all else.

Don't be afraid to use more heat when relevant. It leads to more browning!

If salt isn't rounding out your dish, try adding acid (citrus or vinegar).

Hold your knife properly and protect those fingers.

Especially if you aren't familiar with them, taste every individual ingredient before adding them to a recipe. There's nothing worse than making a beautiful, fresh pesto, only to discover you've added a sharp, bitter olive oil that ruins everything.

Season frequently and from higher up to ensure a more even distribution of seasonings.

Season and taste early and often. Then do it all again. Make that your motto in the kitchen.

Don't serve hot food on cold plates. Nor vice versa.

Let the food cook itself. We all know the overly-confident grill dad who flips the steak every two seconds. Leave it alone. The best cooks let the ingredients do the work.

Don't overcrowd your pan, especially if you're trying to brown something. It prevents the liquid from turning to steam and escaping, and instead swirls between the food in the pan and begins to steam it.

Place a damp kitchen towel under your cutting board for safety to prevent slippage.

QR CODE LIBRARY

Scan to learn how to . . .

**hold a
chef's knife**

**season
properly**

flambé

**cut lemon
wedges**

butter baste

**store
fresh herbs**

**make pasta
dough**

**make a
piping bag**

**form
bagel dough**

shred chicken

**roll an
egg roll**

**make a
smash patty**

**remove
membrane
from ribs**

**make
browned butter**

**cook a lobster
and remove
lobster meat**

**pronounce
"gnocchi"**

flip a tahdig

**lift focaccia
dough**

**accordion-slice
cucumbers**

fold a burrito

FUNDA MENTALS

YOU MUST LEARN THE RULES BEFORE YOU CAN BREAK THEM.

HOMEMADE FLAKY SALT

YIELD
2 cups

PREP TIME
5 minutes

COOK TIME
3 minutes

Salt is part of nearly every meal, so why not make it exciting? I started Osmo Salt for this very reason, but here's how to make it at home.

1 cup (250g) **kosher salt**
4 cups (960ml) **water**

1 In a medium pot, whisk together the salt and water. Bring the mixture to a boil over high heat until the salt dissolves and the water is no longer cloudy, about 3 minutes.

2 Remove the pot from the heat and evenly distribute the mixture among several wide, shallow pans.

3 Place the pans by a window and leave for several days to allow the water to evaporate. Make sure the pans are in a location where they won't be touched or moved.

4 Once the water has completely evaporated, scrape the salt from the pans and enjoy the fun crystals. Store the salt in an airtight container.

BROWN SUGAR

We've all run out of brown sugar at some point. The next time it happens to you, check your pantry. You probably already have everything you need to make brown sugar at home. It's actually just one ingredient: sugar. It's regular sugar combined with molasses, which is also derived from sugar cane.

YIELD
1 cup

PREP TIME
5 minutes

COOK TIME
none

1 cup (198g) **granulated sugar**
1–2 tsp **molasses**

1   In a medium bowl, combine the sugar and molasses. Use 1 teaspoon of molasses for light brown sugar and 2 teaspoons for dark brown sugar.

2   Using a fork or your fingers, mix until the molasses has been fully incorporated. (You can also use a stand mixer with a paddle attachment.)

3   Transfer the brown sugar to an airtight container for storage. Add a slice of white bread to the container to help keep the sugar soft.

TIP   For breakfast, I love to sprinkle brown sugar over a grapefruit half and then torch or broil it. I call it a grapefruit brûlée, and the sweetness cuts the acidity to make for a delicious treat.

QUICK PICKLING

YIELD
2 pint-size jars

PREP TIME
10 minutes

COOK TIME
3 minutes

In a pickle? My quick-pickle method is here to help. Along with extending the shelf life of food, pickling totally transforms the flavor of any given ingredient. Cucumbers and red onions are traditional, though I love pickling all sorts of fruits and veggies ranging from green beans to grapes and strawberries.

1½ cups (360ml) **white vinegar**

1½ cups (360ml) **water**

3 tbsp **granulated sugar**

2 tbsp **kosher salt**

seasonings of choice (such as citrus zest, spices, herbs, etc.)

1lb (454g) **vegetables** or **fruits**

1 In a medium saucepan over medium-high heat, combine the vinegar, water, sugar, salt, and seasonings. Bring to a boil and cook until the sugar has dissolved. Remove the saucepan from the heat.

2 Pack the vegetables or fruits into pint-size Mason jars and add the hot brine to cover. Allow the contents of the jars to cool completely.

3 Secure the lids and refrigerate until the pickles reach your desired flavor profile. Some vegetables are ready immediately upon cooling (for example, thin and porous produce, such as onions), while others might take longer. Most pickled vegetables can be stored in the refrigerator for up to 2 months.

TIP Which seasonings and herbs to use depends heavily upon the chosen fruits or vegetables, although I particularly love adding peppercorns, mustard seeds, lemon zest, or fresh dill.

AGED VANILLA EXTRACT

YIELD
1 cup

PREP TIME
3 minutes + 1 year to age

COOK TIME
none

My vanilla extract's name is Charles. He's two-and-a-half years old and counting. I plan on cultivating the world's oldest bottle of vanilla extract and passing it down to my descendants for generations to come.

6 **vanilla beans**
1 cup (240ml) **vodka** or **bourbon**

1 Using a paring knife, slit the vanilla beans lengthwise and peel them open, exposing the small black seeds inside.

2 Place the vanilla beans upright in a tight-sealing 8-ounce (240ml) bottle. Make sure they can fit vertically without bending when closing the lid. Add enough vodka or bourbon to cover the vanilla beans.

3 Tightly close the lid and set aside a minimum of 3 months—but for best flavor 6 to 12 months—out of direct sunlight. Shake every few weeks to create optimal extract.

4 As you use your vanilla extract, you can top it off with more vodka or bourbon.

TIP Aged vanilla extract is a creative, thoughtful, and easy holiday gift, and it will last more or less forever. If you'd like to continue infusing flavor with beans, they'll need to be replaced about once each year. As long as the vanilla still smells good, it's okay to continue using.

SIMPLE HOMEMADE BUTTER

YIELD
1 cup

PREP TIME
15 minutes

COOK TIME
none

I can't believe it's not butter! All jokes aside, this *is* butter. Really, really great butter. All you're doing is overwhipping whipped cream. It's that easy.

2 cups (480ml) **heavy cream**
¼ tsp **kosher salt**
favorite add-ins (optional)

1 Add the heavy cream to a food processor (a blender or stand mixer with a whisk attachment will also work). Blend on high until the cream separates into yellow butter and cloudy buttermilk, about 10 minutes.

2 Pour off and reserve the buttermilk for another use, if desired. Pour in cold water and agitate the butter until the water becomes cloudy, then repeat this twice more or until the water runs clear.

3 To work the butter and remove the remaining moisture, press the butter up against the side of the bowl with the back of a wooden spoon, pouring off the water as it separates from the butter. Do this until all of the water has been removed.

4 Season the butter with salt. You can also add other ingredients you'd like. If you've properly removed the buttermilk, the butter will keep refrigerated for 2 to 3 weeks in an airtight container, or frozen for up to 9 months in a tightly covered dish.

TIPS Reserved buttermilk can be refrigerated in an airtight container for up to 2 weeks. It's great for brining chicken!

Make a fancy compound butter by adding other ingredients in step 4, such as fresh herbs, garlic, or cinnamon sugar. Use plastic wrap to roll the butter into a log, and refrigerate for 2 to 3 hours before cutting the butter into circular portions.

PERFECT JAMMY EGGS

YIELD
6 eggs

PREP TIME
10 minutes

COOK TIME
6½ minutes

Eggs cooked for about 6½ minutes have perfectly set whites and jammy–if not slightly runny–yolks. If properly executed, they're a remarkable *eggsperience*.

6 **large eggs**

1 Fill a large saucepan halfway with cold water (it should be deep enough to cover the eggs when they are added) and bring to a boil over medium-high heat.

2 Using a slotted spoon, lower the eggs into the water one at a time—work quickly so they all cook for the same amount of time. Cook for about 6½ minutes, uncovered, adjusting the heat as necessary to keep the water gently boiling throughout.

3 In a large bowl, make an ice bath by combining cold water and ice cubes. Place the bowl near the saucepan of boiling water.

4 When 6½ minutes have passed, remove the eggs from the boiling water with a slotted spoon and immediately submerge them in the ice bath.

5 Chill the eggs until just slightly warm, and then test one to see how they're cooked. If you'd like your eggs firmer, simply remove them from the ice bath and the residual heat will continue cooking them. If you're happy with the consistency, allow them to sit in the ice bath until barely warm and eat as you desire.

ROTISSERIE CHICKEN STOCK

YIELD
4 quarts (3.8 liters)

PREP TIME
5 minutes

COOK TIME
7 hours

My love for rotisserie chicken has left me with many chicken carcasses. Save all your scraps—veggies, herbs, bones, Parmesan cheese rinds—and make an amazing multipurpose stock every few months.

1 **rotisserie chicken carcass**
1 **garlic head,** halved
2 **small yellow onions,** quartered
3 **carrots,** roughly chopped
4 **celery stalks,** roughly chopped
1 tsp **whole black peppercorns**
3 **bay leaves**
5 quarts (4.7 liters) **water**
kosher salt, to taste

1   In a large pot over medium-high heat, combine the chicken carcass, garlic, onions, carrots, celery, peppercorns, bay leaves, and water. (This is also when you can add any other veggie scraps!) Bring to a boil, then reduce the heat to medium-low and simmer uncovered for at least 3 hours.

2   During cooking, occasionally use a spoon to skim off any foam that rises to the top and add water as needed to keep the ingredients covered. After simmering for 3 hours, strain out and discard the solids. Season with salt to taste.

3   Use immediately, or cool completely and transfer to an airtight container for storage. Broth can be refrigerated for up to 1 week or frozen for up to 3 months. I like to freeze it in ice cube trays for easy use in recipes.

TIPS   The longer you simmer your stock, the more the liquid will reduce and the more concentrated the flavor will become. For a rich, concentrated stock, strain the solids after simmering for 3 hours and continue to simmer and reduce for 1 to 2 hours more.

Stock is a great opportunity to improvise and play around with what you have on hand. You can add other types of vegetables or aromatics–fennel, leeks, and fresh herbs are all great additions. However, steer clear of green bell peppers (they can add bitterness) and members of the cabbage family, like broccoli and kale.

FRESH RICOTTA CHEESE

YIELD
2 cups

PREP TIME
20 minutes + 15 minutes to drain

COOK TIME
22 minutes

Yes, you can make homemade cheese in just minutes. Start by making a simple whole milk ricotta—the only special equipment needed is cheesecloth—then elevate it by making a luxurious whipped version, perfect for serving over toast with honey.

8 cups (1.9 liters) **whole milk** (not ultra-pasteurized)

½ tsp **kosher salt**

3 tbsp freshly squeezed **lemon juice**

1 Lightly dampen a cheesecloth with water and fold 3 to 4 times. Place the cheesecloth in a colander and place the colander over a medium plastic or glass bowl. Set aside.

2 To make the whole milk ricotta, in a large heavy-bottomed saucepan, warm the milk over medium heat. Clip an instant-read thermometer to the saucepan. Using a wooden spoon, stir in the salt. Cook, stirring occasionally, for 20 minutes or until the temperature reaches 185°F (85°C). Steam and small bubbles should surround the edges of the milk.

3 Reduce the heat to low and add the lemon juice. Stir constantly for about 2 minutes. Remove the saucepan from the heat, cover, and let sit for 20 minutes. Do not move the saucepan.

4 Strain the milk mixture through the cheesecloth and allow to sit and drain for 5 to 15 minutes or until it reaches your desired consistency. Transfer the ricotta to an airtight container and refrigerate for up to 7 days.

TIP   If the mixture doesn't curdle when you add the lemon juice, double check that it is simmering and then add more lemon juice, 1 teaspoon at a time, until the reaction occurs. You don't want to over-agitate the mixture—the goal is just to incorporate the acid, then let the curd float to the top.

VARIATION   To make **Whipped Ricotta,** add 1½ cups (340g) of whole milk ricotta to a blender. With the blender running on low speed, slowly drizzle in ¼ cup (60ml) of extra-virgin olive oil and blend until smooth and creamy. Transfer the whipped ricotta to an airtight container and refrigerate for up to 7 days. Enjoy over toast with honey, ground nutmeg, and fresh berries, or however you'd like.

CARAMELIZED ONIONS

YIELD
4 cups

PREP TIME
10 minutes

COOK TIME
55 minutes

Cooking breaks down and caramelizes the sugars in onions, resulting in a sweet, rich flavor. By adding some additional sugar and baking soda, you'll achieve an even deeper caramelization and a sweeter, more robust flavor.

6 medium **yellow onions,** thinly sliced

¾ cup (180ml) + 1 tbsp **water,** divided

1 tbsp **vegetable oil**

2 tbsp **unsalted butter**

¾ tsp **kosher salt**

3 tbsp **granulated sugar**

⅛ tsp **baking soda**

1 In a large nonstick skillet over high heat, combine the onions, ¾ cup (180ml) of water, oil, butter, and salt. Cook for 15 minutes or until the water has evaporated and the onions begin to sizzle.

2 Reduce the heat to medium. Add the sugar and continue to cook for 30 minutes, stirring for 30 seconds on and 30 seconds off. Adjust the heat as necessary. You're looking for dark golden caramelization, and a few black spots here and there are good.

3 In a small bowl, combine the baking soda and the remaining 1 tablespoon of water. Stir this mixture into the onions and cook for 5 minutes more, stirring constantly, or until caramelized to your liking.

4 Remove the skillet from the heat and transfer the onions to a bowl. Enjoy immediately or refrigerate in an airtight container for up to 5 days.

BROWNED BUTTER

YIELD
1½ cups

PREP TIME
none

COOK TIME
5 minutes

Slightly sweet and nutty with a complex flavor, browned butter is made by toasting the existing milk solids in regular butter. I've added a bit of extra milk powder to further amplify the flavor. Use browned butter in baked goods or drizzle it over fried eggs, vegetables, meat, or seafood.

1½ cups (339g) **unsalted butter,** cubed

⅓ cup (48g) **dry milk powder** (optional)

1   In a medium saucepan, melt the butter over medium-low heat.

2   Whisk in the milk powder (if using) and cook for 3 minutes or until the milk solids become a golden brown color, stirring constantly.

3   Remove the saucepan from the heat—the mixture will continue toasting once off the heat—and, about 30 seconds before you feel it's perfectly golden brown, pour the mixture into a heatproof bowl, scraping any extra bits of milk solids from the pan. Browned butter can be used immediately or refrigerated until ready to use.

TIP   Added milk powder is not necessary to achieve browned butter, but it does result in more browned milk solids, and therefore, increased flavor.

HOW TO MAKE
BROWNED BUTTER

PASTA DOUGH

Fresh pasta is easy. And the taste and mouthfeel are an experience unlike that of any boxed dry pasta you've had. Use this dough to make French & Italian Lasagna (page 170) or Ricotta Ravioli (page 174).

YIELD
14 ounces (397g)

PREP TIME
50 minutes

COOK TIME
3 to 5 minutes

---

2 cups (232g) **00 flour** or
  all-purpose flour
2 **large eggs**
4 **egg yolks**

---

1 Place the flour on a wooden cutting board. Make a well in the middle using the bottom of a bowl or measuring cup.

2 Crack the eggs into the well and add the egg yolks. Whisk the eggs, then slowly incorporate the surrounding flour until well combined. It should feel like very firm Play-Doh. If the dough seems too dry or crumbly, add 1 to 2 tablespoons of cold water. If the dough feels too wet, add a light touch of flour.

3 Knead the dough for about 10 minutes or until nice and smooth. Form the dough into a ball.

4 Wrap the dough tightly in plastic wrap and refrigerate for at least 30 minutes. It can be refrigerated for up to 2 days before rolling out.

5 Divide the dough into four pieces of equal size. Using a pasta machine, roll and cut the dough as desired. You can also use a rolling pin and cut the pasta by hand.

6 To cook, bring a large pot of well-salted water to a gentle boil. Add the pasta and cook for 3 to 5 minutes or until it floats. Drain and serve as desired.

TIP Be sure to use enough flour when rolling and before cooking so your dough doesn't stick.

HOW TO MAKE
PASTA DOUGH

ROASTED + TOASTED PESTO

YIELD
1 to 1½ cups

PREP TIME
5 minutes

COOK TIME
5 minutes

This is an easy recipe—but nonetheless one that will convince those eating it that you know your way around a kitchen. Despite the fact that I've made this many times, my reaction every time is the same proud smile.

⅓ cup (47g) **pine nuts**

¾ cup (180ml) **extra-virgin olive oil,** divided

3 **garlic cloves**

2 cups (50g) **fresh basil leaves,** packed

½ cup (50g) freshly grated **Parmesan cheese**

kosher salt and freshly ground **black pepper,** to taste

TIPS   When you're ready to use the pesto, don't add it to a hot pan. Instead, cook your pasta first, transfer the hot pasta to a serving bowl, and then stir in the pesto.

To mix things up, try replacing the pine nuts with pistachio nuts. It's quite common in Sicily and results in a creamy, nutty alternative I love.

1   In a medium skillet, toast the pine nuts over medium heat for 2 to 3 minutes until lightly golden brown and fragrant. (Remove the pine nuts just before you think they're done; they'll continue to toast even after they're off the heat.) Transfer the pine nuts to a small bowl and set aside.

2   In the same pan, heat ¼ cup (60ml) of olive oil over medium heat until warm. Add the garlic and sauté for 2 to 3 minutes until lightly golden brown and aromatic, stirring frequently. Immediately pour both the garlic and oil into a small bowl and set aside.

3   Bring a pot of water to a rolling boil over high heat. In a large bowl, prepare an ice bath by combining cold water and ice. Place the ice bath near the pot of boiling water.

4   Blanch the basil by submerging it in the boiling water for 15 seconds, then immediately plunge the basil into the ice bath. Working quickly, remove the basil from the ice bath and use a kitchen towel to press as much excess water from the basil as possible.

5   Before blending, ensure all ingredients have cooled to room temperature. In a blender, combine the blanched basil, toasted pine nuts, and garlic (with cooking oil), along with the Parmesan and the remaining ½ cup (120ml) of olive oil. Pulse until the pesto reaches the consistency of your liking. Taste and add salt and pepper as needed.

6   Use immediately, or transfer to an airtight container and refrigerate for up to 5 days.

GARLICKY CROUTONS

YIELD
6 to 7 cups

PREP TIME
3 minutes

COOK TIME
10 to 12 minutes

I can't tell if I like croutons (broken into breadcrumbs) better as a simple snack or crumbled over a salad or pasta. Either way, they're a fantastic way to utilize stale bread while simultaneously providing texture and excitement.

1 loaf of **sourdough bread**
¼ cup (60ml) **extra-virgin olive oil**
½ tbsp **garlic powder**
kosher salt and freshly ground
  black pepper, to taste

1   Preheat the oven to 400°F (200°C). Line a baking sheet with parchment paper.

2   Use a serrated knife to cut the bread into evenly sized cubes. If your bread is already hard and brittle (which mine often is), do your best to break it up into smaller bits.

3   On the prepared baking sheet, combine the bread cubes, olive oil, and garlic powder. Season with salt and pepper to taste. Mix well.

4   Place the baking sheet in the oven and bake for 10 to 12 minutes or until the croutons are golden brown, shaking the pan every 4 to 5 minutes.

5   Remove the pan from the oven and allow the croutons to cool completely before using.

TIP   You can make this recipe with other types of bread, but nothing compares to sourdough croutons. With that said, you can get creative and use cornbread, brioche, or even sandwich bread. Stale bread is great for making croutons, but the harder it is, the more difficult it becomes to cut into cubes.

SAUCE LIBRARY

These easy-to-make sauces will come in handy for a variety of uses.

RANCH DRESSING

Ranch has always been my favorite dressing (no offense, blue cheese dressing lovers). This creamy buttermilk sauce is filled with fresh herbs and can complement a variety of foods.

YIELD
1 cup

PREP TIME
10 minutes

COOK TIME
none

¼ cup (56g) **mayonnaise**
⅓ cup (75g) **sour cream**
¼ cup (60ml) **buttermilk**
1½ tbsp minced **fresh dill**
½ tbsp chopped **fresh chives**
¼ tsp **garlic powder**
¼ tsp **onion powder**
½ tbsp freshly squeezed **lemon juice**
kosher salt and freshly ground **black pepper,** to taste

In a medium bowl, whisk together all the ingredients.

CREAMY HONEY MUSTARD-BBQ SAUCE

The popular Chick-Fil-A sauce is secretly just a well-balanced mixture of barbecue, honey mustard, and ranch. This quick copycat version is easy to make at home.

YIELD
1 cup

PREP TIME
5 minutes

COOK TIME
none

⅔ cup (150g) **mayonnaise**
¼ cup (72g) **barbecue sauce**
¼ cup (84g) **honey**
2 tbsp **yellow mustard**
2 tsp freshly squeezed **lemon juice**

In a medium bowl, whisk together all the ingredients.

SPECIAL SAUCE

Everybody has their own version of special sauce, typically used to amplify a good burger. This versatile sauce pairs wonderfully with burgers, tacos, and more.

YIELD
1 cup

PREP TIME
10 minutes

COOK TIME
none

½ cup (112g) **mayonnaise**
¼ cup (68g) **ketchup**
⅓ cup (80g) finely chopped **dill pickles**
1 tbsp **yellow mustard**
2 tsp **Worcestershire sauce**
1 tbsp freshly squeezed **lemon juice**
¼ tsp **smoked paprika**
¼ tsp **garlic powder**
kosher salt, to taste

In a medium bowl, whisk together all the ingredients.

BUFFALO SAUCE

Homemade buffalo sauce is buttery and creamy, and allows you to better control the heat levels. I've found good bottled buffalo sauces, but never anything great, so I started making my own several years ago.

YIELD
1 cup

PREP TIME
5 minutes

COOK TIME
3 minutes

⅔ cup (160ml) **hot sauce**

1½ tbsp **white vinegar**

¼ tsp **Worcestershire sauce**

½ cup (113g) **unsalted butter**, at room temperature, cubed

pinch of **ground cayenne**

pinch of **garlic powder**

kosher salt, to taste

---

1 In a small pot over medium heat, combine the hot sauce, vinegar, and Worcestershire sauce. As soon as it starts to bubble, immediately transfer the mixture to a blender.

2 With the blender on medium speed, slowly add the butter. A blender is important to ensure you get a proper emulsion, where everything is combined into one smooth and uniform sauce.

3 Transfer to a bowl and season to taste with cayenne pepper, garlic powder, and salt.

BARBECUE SAUCE

Barbecue sauce is well rounded and flavorful, hitting on sweet, sour, spicy, and smoky notes. Use this recipe as a foundation, and adjust the seasonings in order to achieve the barbecue sauce of your dreams.

YIELD
1⅓ cups

PREP TIME
5 minutes

COOK TIME
8 minutes

---

1 cup (272g) **ketchup**

½ cup (107g) **Brown Sugar** (page 25)

¼ cup (60ml) **water**

¼ cup (60ml) **apple cider vinegar**

1 tbsp **unsalted butter**

1 tbsp **Worcestershire sauce**

½ tbsp **dry mustard**

2 tsp **smoked paprika**

1 tsp **kosher salt**

¾ tsp freshly ground **black pepper**

¼ tsp **onion powder**

¼ tsp **garlic powder**

pinch of **ground cayenne**

---

1 In a small pot, combine all the ingredients and bring to a low boil over medium heat.

2 Reduce the heat to medium-low and cook for 5 to 7 minutes, whisking often, until the desired consistency has been reached.

SNACKS + DIPS

A LIFE WITHOUT SNACKS IS NO LIFE AT ALL.

CRISPY ARTICHOKES
WITH TARTAR SAUCE

YIELD
5 to 6 servings

PREP TIME
12 minutes

COOK TIME
15 minutes

I don't know what it is about artichokes that makes me love them the way I do. But you just can't beat a crispy fried 'choke dipped in a homemade tartar sauce.

4 cups (960ml) **high-heat cooking oil,** for frying

¾ cup (90g) **all-purpose flour**

¾ cup (114g) **potato starch**

1 tbsp **garlic powder**

1 tbsp **onion powder**

1 tsp **baking powder**

2 tsp **kosher salt,** plus more to finish

½ tsp freshly ground **black pepper**

2 (14oz [397g]) cans of **quartered artichoke hearts,** drained

FOR THE TARTAR SAUCE

¾ cup (180g) **mayonnaise**

2 tbsp minced **cornichons**

2 tbsp minced **capers**

1 tsp **cornichon brine**

½ tsp **Worcestershire sauce**

1 **scallion,** minced

1 small **shallot,** minced

1 tsp freshly squeezed **lemon juice**

½ tsp freshly ground **black pepper**

1 Prepare a rimmed baking sheet with a wire rack. In a Dutch oven, heat the oil over medium-high heat to 375°F (190°C).

2 To make the tartar sauce, in a small bowl, combine all the ingredients. Mix well. Set aside or refrigerate until ready to serve.

3 In a large bowl, whisk together the flour, potato starch, garlic powder, onion powder, baking powder, salt, and pepper. Add the artichoke hearts and toss to coat evenly.

4 Working in 2 to 3 batches, add the artichokes to the hot oil and stir upon dropping them in to ensure they don't stick to one another. Fry for 5 to 7 minutes or until golden brown.

5 Transfer the artichokes to the wire rack and immediately sprinkle with salt. Serve with the tartar sauce.

TIP Cornichons are those cute mini pickles you've seen on fancy charcuterie boards!

BACON-WRAPPED DATES

YIELD
16 dates

PREP TIME
10 minutes

COOK TIME
20 minutes

A four-ingredient recipe shouldn't taste this good. The combination of chewy and crispy on the outside and sweet and savory on the inside makes for the perfect party food. Blue cheese can be used instead of goat cheese, and if you want to go dairy-free, try stuffing the dates with almonds.

8 slices of thin-cut **bacon**

16 **Medjool dates**

2½oz (70g) **goat cheese**, softened

¼ cup (78g) **pure maple syrup**

balsamic glaze (optional), to garnish

1   Preheat the oven to 350°F (175°C). Line a baking sheet with parchment paper.

2   Cut each piece of bacon in half and set aside. (If the bacon is too long, it will be too thick when wrapped around a date and won't crisp throughout.)

3   Slice the dates lengthwise to create an opening down the middle. Remove and discard the pits.

4   Fill a piping bag with goat cheese. Cut off the tip of the bag and pipe the cheese into the dates, pressing the dates to close them around the cheese.

5   Wrap each date with half a bacon slice and secure with a toothpick. Place the bacon-wrapped dates on the prepared baking sheet.

6   Bake for 10 minutes. Remove the sheet from the oven and brush each date with maple syrup.

7   Return the sheet to the oven and bake for 10 to 15 minutes more or until the bacon is crisped to your liking.

8   Remove the sheet from the oven and allow the dates to cool for several minutes. Drizzle with balsamic glaze before serving, if desired.

HOW TO MAKE
A PIPING BAG

CRUNCHY SNACKING CHICKPEAS

YIELD
2 cups

PREP TIME
3 minutes

COOK TIME
25 minutes

The best snacks are those that taste unhealthy but are, in fact, good for you. Ta-da!

2 (15oz [425g]) cans of **chickpeas**
⅓ cup (80ml) **avocado oil**
½ tsp **smoked paprika**
¼ tsp **garlic powder**
¼ tsp **onion powder**
sea salt and freshly ground
   black pepper, to taste

1   Preheat the oven to 425°F (220°C). Line a baking sheet with parchment paper. Drain and rinse the chickpeas. Pat dry with paper towels.

2   In a large cast-iron skillet, heat the avocado oil over medium-high heat. Add the chickpeas and cook for 5 to 8 minutes, stirring occasionally, until they are blistered and slightly charred.

3   Drain any remaining oil and transfer the chickpeas to the prepared baking sheet. Bake for 17 to 20 minutes until light golden brown and crispy.

4   Remove from the oven and sprinkle the paprika, garlic powder, onion powder, salt, and pepper over the chickpeas. Toss to coat them evenly in the spices.

5   Return the chickpeas to the oven for 5 minutes more. Cool slightly before serving. When cool, chickpeas can be stored in a glass jar at room temperature for up to 1 week.

CRAB + ARTICHOKE DIP
WITH OLD BAY CROSTINI

YIELD
8 to 10 servings

PREP TIME
10 minutes

COOK TIME
30 minutes

This recipe builds on the traditional pairing of crab and Old Bay—a classic Maryland crab seasoning. My grandpa taught my brothers and me to catch blue crabs when we were little, so this dish always reminds me of him.

8oz (227g) **cream cheese,** softened

½ cup (114g) **sour cream**

½ cup (112g) **mayonnaise**

¾ cup (85g) shredded **mild cheddar**

kosher salt and freshly ground **black pepper,** to taste

½ tsp **Old Bay seasoning,** plus more for crostini

dash of **Worcestershire sauce**

zest and juice of 1 **lemon,** divided

1 (14oz [397g]) can of **quartered artichoke hearts,** drained and roughly chopped

1lb (454g) **jumbo lump crab meat**

1 tbsp **unsalted butter,** softened

¾ cup (85g) shredded **mozzarella**

2 **scallions,** thinly sliced, divided

chopped **fresh chives,** to garnish

crostini, to serve

1 Preheat the oven to 400°F (200°C).

2 In a medium bowl, combine the cream cheese, sour cream, mayonnaise, and cheddar. Season well with salt and pepper, and stir in the Old Bay seasoning, Worcestershire sauce, and 1 to 2 tablespoons of lemon juice. Mix well.

3 Gently stir in the artichokes and crab meat, mixing just until incorporated.

4 Using a pastry brush, coat the interior of a 9-inch (23cm) cast-iron skillet with the butter. Add the filling, then sprinkle with the lemon zest, mozzarella, and half of the scallions.

5 Place the skillet in the oven and bake for 25 to 30 minutes or until bubbling and golden brown on top. Remove the skillet from the oven and top with the chives and the remaining scallions.

6 Using a small mesh sieve, lightly dust the crostini with Old Bay seasoning. (Dust and taste one before dusting the rest, as Old Bay is quite strong.) Serve immediately.

TIPS   If you're able to, I highly recommend cooking the dip on a grill instead of in the oven for a bit of smoky flavor.

Buy high-quality crostini—crunchy, buttery ones sliced from actual bread. Or better yet, make your own. For **Homemade Crostini,** thinly slice a ficelle (thin baguette), spread on a parchment-lined baking sheet, and drizzle with olive oil, salt, and pepper. Bake at 400°F (200°C) for 8 to 10 minutes or until crispy and golden brown.

WATERMELON + HALLOUMI SKEWERS

YIELD
4 to 6 skewers

PREP TIME
15 minutes

COOK TIME
15 minutes

To me, this combination is far superior to watermelon and feta. There's a delicious contrast between the sweet, juicy watermelon and the warm, gooey griddled halloumi.

8oz (227g) **halloumi,** cut into 1-inch (2.5cm) cubes, at room temperature

2 cups (300g) 1-inch- (2.5cm) cubed **watermelon**

1–2 tbsp **extra-virgin olive oil**

sea salt and freshly ground **black pepper,** to taste

1 tbsp **honey**

4 **mint leaves,** whole or torn

4 **basil leaves,** whole or torn

1 **lemon,** to grate for zest

1   Preheat the grill to medium-high, about 400°F (200°C). Make sure the grates are clean and oiled so the halloumi doesn't stick. While you slice the halloumi and watermelon, soak 4 to 6 wooden skewers in water so they don't catch fire on the grill.

2   Thread the halloumi and watermelon on the wooden skewers, placing about 2 pieces of watermelon for every 1 piece of halloumi. (The halloumi can sometimes crack; be careful.)

3   Brush the halloumi and watermelon with olive oil. Season with salt and pepper to taste.

4   Place the skewers on the grill and cook for 3 minutes per side. Do not touch or rotate the skewers until the halloumi has softened and developed grill marks. If they are still sticking, they are not ready to flip yet; if they begin to burn, reduce the temperature of the grill or move to a cooler spot on the grill.

5   Remove the skewers from the grill and immediately brush with a light coating of honey.

6   Place the skewers on a serving platter and sprinkle the mint and basil over the top. Grate lemon zest over the top before serving.

TIP   Slap or spank the watermelons in the supermarket to choose the best one. It should vibrate and have a nice hollow sound.

CARAMELIZED ONION DIP

YIELD
5 cups

PREP TIME
10 minutes

COOK TIME
50 minutes

Onion soup mix and sour cream . . . let's be honest, we've all done it (or seen somebody do it for a party or potluck), and it's delicious. But you haven't lived until you've had the real thing.

4 medium **yellow onions,** chopped

⅓ cup (80ml) + 1 tbsp **water,** divided

4 tsp **unsalted butter**

2 tsp **vegetable oil**

½ tsp **kosher salt**

2 tbsp **granulated sugar**

⅛ tsp **baking soda**

1 cup (227g) **sour cream**

8oz (225g) **cream cheese,** softened

⅓ cup (75g) **mayonnaise**

2 **scallions,** thinly sliced

½ tsp **onion powder**

½ tsp **Worcestershire sauce**

kosher salt and freshly **ground black pepper,** to taste

chopped **fresh parsley,** to garnish

potato chips (optional), to serve

1 In a large nonstick skillet over high heat, combine the onions, ⅓ cup (80ml) of water, butter, oil, and salt. Cook for 15 minutes or until the water has evaporated and the onions begin to sizzle.

2 Reduce the heat to medium. Add the sugar and continue to cook for 30 minutes, stirring for 30 seconds on and 30 seconds off. Adjust the heat as necessary. You're looking for dark golden caramelization, and a few black spots here and there are good.

3 In a small bowl, combine the baking soda and the remaining 1 tablespoon of water. Stir this into the onions and cook for 5 minutes, stirring constantly, or until caramelized to your liking. Remove the skillet from the heat and cool to room temperature.

4 In a medium bowl, combine the onions with the sour cream, cream cheese, mayonnaise, scallions, onion powder, and Worcestershire sauce. Season with salt and pepper to taste.

5 Garnish with parsley and enjoy immediately with potato chips, or refrigerate for up to 4 days in a covered container.

TIP Serve with chips, pretzels, veggies, crackers, crostinis, or whatever you'd like.

PINE NUT HUMMUS

YIELD
3 cups

PREP TIME
15 minutes

COOK TIME
20 minutes

One of my food science courses in college occasionally referenced recipes from America's Test Kitchen, which often utilize simple scientific practices to create better food. I've adapted their recipe to make an extraordinarily creamy, flavorful hummus.

2 (15oz [425g]) cans of **chickpeas,** rinsed and drained

½ tsp **baking soda**

6 cups (1.4 liters) **water**

3 **garlic cloves**

juice of 2 **lemons**

1 tbsp **kosher salt**

5 **ice cubes**

¼ tsp **ground cumin**

½ cup (71g) **toasted pine nuts,** divided

½ cup (128g) **light tahini**

2 tbsp **extra-virgin olive oil,** plus more to garnish

TO GARNISH

freshly ground **black pepper**

ground **sumac**

smoked paprika

zest of 1 **lemon**

1. In a medium saucepan, combine the chickpeas, baking soda, and water. Bring to a boil over medium-high heat, then reduce the heat to low. Simmer for 20 minutes or until the chickpea skins begin floating, stirring every few minutes.

2. Meanwhile, using a garlic press, squeeze the garlic cloves into the bowl of a food processor. Add the lemon juice and salt. Mix well and set aside.

3. Drain the chickpeas and add them to a large bowl of cold water to remove the remaining skins. Discard the skins and drain again.

4. To the food processor, add the chickpeas, ice cubes, cumin, and half the pine nuts. Process for 1 minute, then add the tahini and olive oil. Process for 90 seconds more.

5. For extra creaminess, transfer the hummus to a food mill and push it through. Taste and adjust seasonings as needed.

6. Spread the hummus on a large plate. Drizzle lightly with olive oil and sprinkle with pepper, sumac, and paprika. Grate some lemon zest over the top and finish with the remaining pine nuts before serving.

TIP To make **Homemade Pita Chips,** rub pita bread slices with extra-virgin olive oil, then season with salt and pepper to taste. Bake in the oven at 425°F (220°C) for about 7 minutes or until crispy, flipping halfway.

VIRAL PASTA CHIPS

YIELD
3 cups

PREP TIME
5 minutes

COOK TIME
16 to 24 minutes

If you like pasta, you'll *love* these. It's such an easy snack to prepare, and you can pair it with your favorite sauce for dipping! Try marinara, alfredo, pesto, or vodka sauce.

2 cups (150g) **dry farfalle pasta**

2 tbsp **extra-virgin olive oil**

⅔ cup (67g) freshly grated **Parmesan cheese**

kosher salt and freshly ground **black pepper,** to taste

dipping sauce of choice (optional), to serve

1   Bring a large pot of generously salted water to a boil over high heat. Add the farfalle and cook for 8 to 12 minutes or until al dente. While the pasta cooks, preheat the air fryer to 400°F (200°C).

2   Drain the water and transfer the pasta to a medium bowl. Add the olive oil, Parmesan, salt, and a few generous grinds of pepper. Stir to combine.

3   Add the mixture to the air fryer basket and bake for 12 to 15 minutes, occasionally shaking the basket to ensure the pieces of pasta don't stick to one another, and that they achieve an even browning.

4   Remove the pasta chips from the basket and allow to cool slightly. Serve with your favorite dipping sauce, if desired.

TIP   If you don't use farfalle, choose another pasta shape that will hold a dipping sauce well. Rigatoni is a fun pick.

BREAK FAST

I'M NOT A MORNING PERSON, BUT THIS IS FOOD WORTH WAKING UP FOR.

ORANGE CHOCOLATE PANCAKES

WITH WHIPPED MAPLE BUTTER

I began experimenting with pancake recipes at a young age, playing around with the flavors and textures. Two decades later, my recipe remains largely the same.

YIELD
10 to 12 pancakes

PREP TIME
15 minutes

COOK TIME
15 minutes

1½ cups (360ml) **whole milk**

zest and juice of 1 **orange**, divided

2 cups (240g) **all-purpose flour**

3 tbsp **granulated sugar**

4 tsp **baking powder**

½ tsp **baking soda**

1 tsp **kosher salt**

2 large **eggs**

¼ cup (57g) **unsalted butter,** melted

½ tsp **Aged Vanilla Extract** (page 29)

⅔ cup (113g) **semisweet chocolate chips**

clarified butter, for cooking

FOR THE BUTTER

1 cup (226g) **unsalted butter,** softened

1 cup (114g) sifted **confectioners' sugar**

⅓ cup (104g) **pure maple syrup,** plus more to serve

1   To make the whipped maple butter, in the bowl of an electric mixer, beat the butter until light and fluffy. Do NOT overwhip! Add the confectioners' sugar and maple syrup. Beat until well combined, soft, and creamy. Set aside.

2   In a medium bowl, combine the milk and 2 tablespoons of orange juice. Let sit for 5 minutes.

3   In a large bowl, whisk together the flour, sugar, baking powder, baking soda, and salt.

4   To the bowl with the milk, add the eggs, butter, vanilla extract, and about 2 teaspoons of orange zest (reserve some zest to garnish). Whisk to combine. Add the wet ingredients to the dry ingredients, along with the chocolate chips, and stir very gently until just barely combined. You want it to be nice and clumpy, as this will result in fluffier pancakes. Let the batter rest for a few minutes as you heat the pan.

5   In a large nonstick skillet, melt ½ teaspoon of clarified butter over medium-low heat until it shimmers. Working in batches, pour the batter onto the skillet in ⅓-cup (80g) portions, making sure not to overcrowd the skillet. Cook for 2 minutes or until the bottoms turn golden brown, then flip and cook for 2 minutes more. Repeat until all the batter is used.

6   Serve warm, topped with the maple butter, more maple syrup, and more orange zest.

TIP   I occasionally chop up some Maple & Lemon Bacon (page 79) and sprinkle it on these pancakes before serving. It's a fun twist and a better combination than you might expect.

CHICKEN SCRAMBLED EGGS

YIELD
4 servings

PREP TIME
3 minutes

COOK TIME
5 to 8 minutes

My grandfather made just two things in the kitchen: crispy rice and scrambled eggs. His secret for eggs? Chicken bouillon seasoning. I've built on his recipe by incorporating some of Gordon Ramsay's famed egg-scrambling techniques.

8 large **eggs**

3 **egg yolks** (optional)

¼ cup (60ml) **half and half**

1½ tbsp **chicken bouillon powder** (Herb Ox recommended)

pinch of freshly ground **black pepper**

1 tbsp **unsalted butter,** chilled

2 tbsp **crème fraîche**

chopped **fresh chives,** to garnish

Homemade Flaky Salt (page 22), to taste

1 In a medium bowl, use a fork to beat together the eggs, egg yolks (if using), half and half, bouillon powder, and pepper until the eggs are well combined but not overmixed.

2 In a medium nonstick skillet over medium heat, melt the butter until lightly foaming. Add the egg mixture and stir continuously with a rubber spatula, scraping around the entire pan, until the eggs begin to clump, about 3 minutes.

3 Reduce the heat to low and continue gently folding the eggs, taking care not to break them apart too much, until they're just slightly wet, about 30 to 60 seconds.

4 Remove the skillet from the heat and fold in the crème fraîche. Transfer the eggs to a plate and sprinkle with chives and flaky salt, or wrap in a fresh Flour Tortilla (page 196).

TIPS The optional extra egg yolks impart a richer flavor and brighter color, but it's not necessary to add them.

Keep in mind that the eggs will continue to cook once removed from heat. If they seem a little underdone beforehand, that's perfect.

Feel free to add an extra dusting of chicken bouillon powder before serving.

EVERYTHING BAGELS

YIELD
8 bagels

PREP TIME
30 minutes + 2 hours to rise

COOK TIME
30 minutes

Whether you're indecisive and want all the toppings or you're just a diehard everything bagel fan like me, I'd like to hope we can all agree that everything is the best flavor. And, if you disagree, you can simply add or omit whatever toppings you'd like!

1½ cups (360ml) **warm water,** plus more as needed

1 tbsp **Brown Sugar** (page 25)

2¼ tsp **active dry yeast**

2 cups (240g) **bread flour**

2 cups (240g) **all-purpose flour**

2½ tsp **kosher salt**

vegetable oil spray, for greasing

1 **egg white**

¼ cup (50g) **granulated sugar**

1 tbsp **baking soda**

FOR THE SEASONING MIX

2 tbsp **poppy seeds**

1 tbsp **white sesame seeds**

1 tbsp **black sesame seeds**

1 tbsp **minced dried onion**

1 tbsp **minced dried garlic**

2 tsp **Homemade Flaky Salt** (page 22)

HOW TO FORM
BAGEL DOUGH

1 To the bowl of a stand mixer, add the warm water and whisk in the brown sugar and yeast. Let sit for 5 minutes or until the yeast activates and becomes foamy.

2 Add the bread flour, all-purpose flour, and kosher salt. Fit the mixer with a dough hook and mix on low speed for 2 minutes. If the dough seems too dry, add 1 to 2 tablespoons of water.

3 Transfer the dough to a clean work surface (lightly flour the surface if needed) and knead by hand for 5 to 6 minutes. Lightly grease a large bowl with vegetable oil spray and add the dough, coating the ball in the oil. Cover with a damp kitchen towel and allow to rise in a warm place for 1 to 2 hours or until the dough doubles in size.

4 Divide the dough into 8 equal pieces, approximately 4 ounces (120g) each. Shape each piece into a ball by pinching down the edges, then roll into a ball and flatten into a disk about 4 inches (10cm) in diameter. Using your thumb and index finger, press a hole through the center of each disk and reshape the dough to make the hole a bit larger, ½ inch (1.25cm). Place the shaped bagels on a baking sheet lined with parchment paper. Cover the dough with a damp kitchen towel and let rest for 30 minutes.

5 Meanwhile, in a small bowl, whisk the egg white with 1 tablespoon of water to make an egg wash. In a medium bowl, combine the seasoning mix ingredients. Set both aside.

6 Preheat the oven to 425°F (220°C). Place a wire rack on a baking sheet and spray with vegetable oil spray.

7 Fill a Dutch oven with about 4 quarts (3.8 liters) of water. Add the granulated sugar and baking soda, and bring to a boil over high heat. Once boiling, add 4 bagels to the water and cook for 30 seconds. Using a slotted spoon, flip the bagels and cook

for 30 seconds more. Place on the prepared wire rack and repeat with the remaining 4 bagels. Keep the water boiling for use in step 9.

8 Brush the top and sides of each bagel with the egg wash, then sprinkle the seasoning mix over the bagels.

9 Place the sheet in the oven. Quickly but carefully, pour about ½ cup (120ml) of boiling water into the bottom of the baking sheet. This will help steam the bagels as they cook.

10 Bake for 20 to 25 minutes or until golden brown, rotating the tray 180 degrees halfway through.

11 Remove the sheet from the oven and allow the bagels to cool before serving.

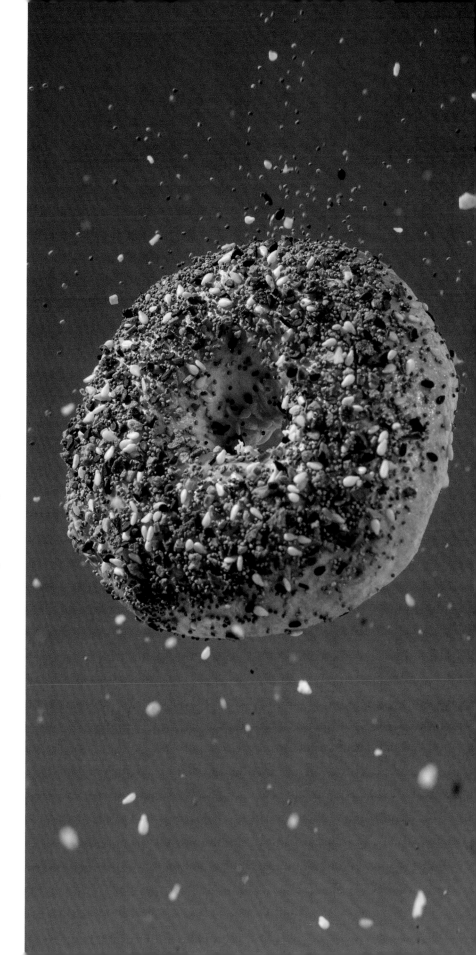

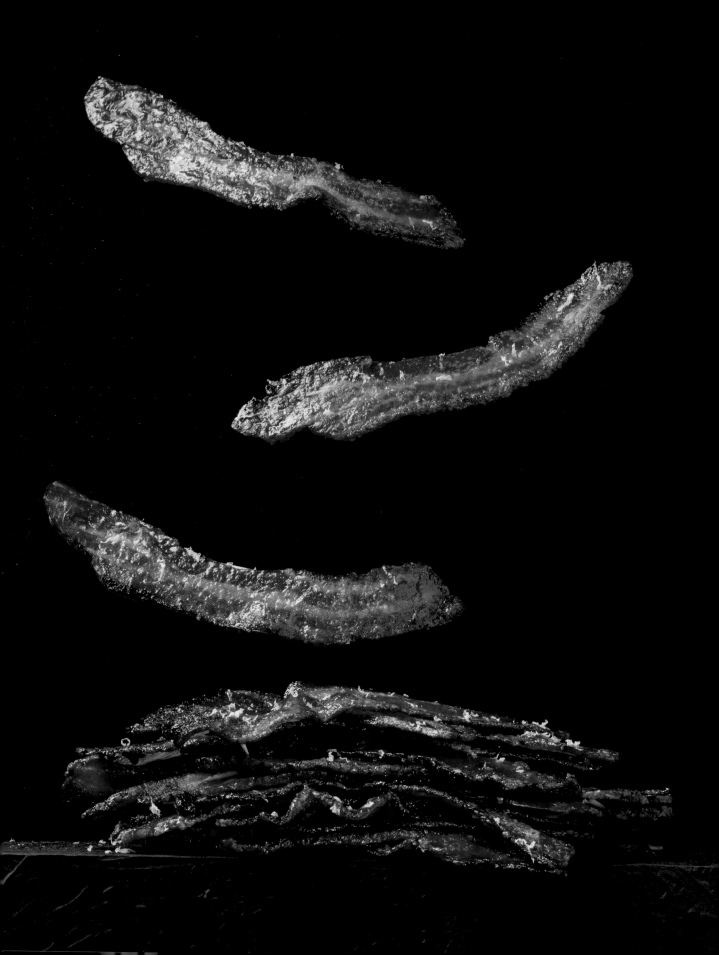

MAPLE + LEMON BACON

YIELD
15 to 20 slices

PREP TIME
10 minutes

COOK TIME
25 to 30 minutes

I love to take ordinary ingredients and adjust them to make them extraordinary. This recipe turns regular bacon into an irresistible masterpiece.

1lb (454g) **uncured bacon**

⅓ cup (104g) **pure maple syrup,** divided

½ cup (107g) **Brown Sugar** (page 25), divided

1 **lemon,** to grate for zest

1 Preheat the oven to 425°F (220°C). Line a baking sheet with foil and place a wire rack on top of the foil.

2 Arrange the bacon evenly across the baking rack. Using a pastry brush, coat the bacon with half of the maple syrup and sprinkle half of the brown sugar over the top.

3 Place the sheet in the oven and bake for about 12 minutes or until the sugar has started to caramelize. Flip the bacon, brush with the remaining maple syrup, and sprinkle with the remaining brown sugar. Bake for 12 to 15 minutes more, depending on your desired crispness.

4 Remove the sheet from the oven. Using a Microplane grater, immediately grate some lemon zest over the top so the zest sticks to the glaze as the bacon cools. Serve immediately.

TIP You should always bake your bacon. It makes for a far better final product. No more stovetop bacon please, unless absolutely necessary.

BENEDICT BREAKFAST SANDWICH

YIELD
2 sandwiches

PREP TIME
15 minutes

COOK TIME
15 minutes

Eggs Benedict is my favorite breakfast order, but I don't love that you need a fork and knife to eat it. Because it's an open-faced sandwich to begin with, I finished the job.

1 tbsp **white vinegar**

2 large **eggs**

2 **English muffins**, sliced

2 tbsp **unsalted butter**

4oz (113g) **smoked salmon** or
2 slices cooked **bacon** or cooked **Canadian bacon**

chopped **fresh chives**, to garnish

1 **lemon**, to grate for zest

FOR THE HOLLANDAISE

3 **egg yolks**

2 tbsp freshly squeezed **lemon juice**

1 tbsp **water**

kosher salt, to taste

pinch of **ground cayenne**

½ cup (113g) **unsalted butter**, softened

TIPS If your hollandaise sauce "breaks" or needs to be revived prior to serving, gradually whisk in some hot water until it reaches the desired consistency.

If you prefer a less runny egg, either cook your poached eggs longer or make Perfect Jammy Eggs (page 33).

1 Preheat the oven to 350°F (175°C).

2 To make the hollandaise sauce, prepare a double boiler by placing a small pot with about ½ inch (1.25cm) of water on the stovetop and place a medium glass bowl over the top. Control the heat to maintain a gentle boil. To the bowl, add the egg yolks, lemon juice, water, salt, and cayenne. Stirring rapidly with a whisk, add the butter a few chunks at a time. If the eggs begin to clump, lift the bowl off the pot for a moment to slow the cooking.

3 Once all the butter has been incorporated, continue stirring for 1 to 2 minutes more or until the sauce has reached your desired thickness. If the sauce begins to curdle or overthicken, add a splash of hot water and continue whisking. Remove the pot from the heat and set aside until ready to assemble the sandwiches.

4 Bring a large pot of water to a boil, then reduce the heat to low. Add the vinegar. Crack 1 egg into a fine-mesh strainer over the sink and swirl to remove and discard the loose egg white. Transfer the egg to a small ramekin. Repeat with the second egg. Using a whisk, swirl the water in the pot to create a vortex. Tip the eggs out of the ramekins into the water, gently continuing the vortex with the whisk as they cook, about 3 minutes. Remove with a slotted spoon and set aside on a plate lined with a paper towel.

5 Spread the cut side of each English muffin half with ½ tablespoon of butter. Heat a medium skillet over medium heat. Add the English muffin halves to the skillet, cut side down, and toast for 3 minutes or until golden brown.

6 To assemble, on each of 2 English muffin halves, place 2 ounces (57g) of salmon, a poached egg, and a dollop of hollandaise sauce. Sprinkle with chives and grate some lemon zest over the top. Close each sandwich by placing an English muffin half on top.

WAFFLE IRON HASH BROWNS

YIELD
8 waffles

PREP TIME
15 minutes + making bacon
and browned butter

COOK TIME
7 minutes

A waffle iron isn't just for waffles. Hash browns cooked on a waffle iron have maximized golden brown crispiness, are easier to make, and aesthetically can't be beat.

2 **large russet potatoes,** about 1½lb (680g) total

2 strips of **Maple & Lemon Bacon** (page 79), finely chopped

1 medium **yellow onion,** finely chopped

2 tbsp **Browned Butter** (page 41)

⅔ cup (75g) freshly grated **cheddar**

1 large **egg,** beaten

2 tbsp **all-purpose flour**

kosher salt and freshly ground **black pepper,** to taste

crème fraîche or **sour cream** (optional), to serve

chopped **scallions** (optional), to garnish

1   In a large pot, cover the potatoes with cold, generously salted water and bring to a boil. Once it reaches a boil, cook for 10 minutes more. Drain, then rinse the potatoes under cold water. Dry the potatoes and grate them into a large bowl.

2   Preheat a waffle iron to medium-high heat. Preheat the oven to 250°F (120°C). Place a wire rack on a rimmed baking sheet.

3   To the large bowl with the potatoes, add the bacon, onion, butter, cheddar, egg, and flour. Season with salt and pepper to taste. Mix well to combine.

4   Spray the hot waffle iron with cooking spray. Add about ¼ cup (60g) of the potato mixture, then quickly spread it and press it down. Close the lid and cook for 7 to 10 minutes or until the potatoes are browned and crispy. After about 5 minutes, once the hash brown is no longer sticking to the waffle iron, you can begin lifting the lid to check for doneness.

5   Transfer the hash brown "waffle" to the prepared baking sheet and place it in the oven to keep warm while you cook the remaining potato mixture.

6   Transfer the warm hash browns to individual serving plates. If desired, top with crème fraîche or sour cream and scallions before serving.

TIPS   Although fresh potatoes will always taste, well, fresher, you can use thawed pre-shredded hash browns, which will also be drier to begin with.

Try topping the hash browns with avocado slices and everything bagel seasoning for a fun take on avocado toast.

ITALIAN BREAKFAST SAUSAGE

YIELD
8 sausage patties

PREP TIME
10 minutes + 8 hours to rest

COOK TIME
8 to 10 minutes

Italian sausage is incredibly versatile, and it certainly doesn't have to be reserved for breakfast. It is, however, delicious with eggs or in a Loaded Breakfast Burrito (page 87).

1 tsp crushed **fennel seeds**

1½ tsp coarsely cracked **black pepper**

1lb (454g) **ground pork**

1 tbsp minced **garlic**

1 tsp **onion powder**

1 tbsp **paprika**

1 tbsp chopped **fresh parsley**

¼ tsp **dried thyme**

¼ tsp **dried rosemary**

¼ tsp **dried oregano**

¼ tsp **dried sage**

1 tbsp **red wine vinegar**

1 tbsp **pure maple syrup**

1 tsp **kosher salt**

1 In a small skillet over medium heat, toast the fennel seeds and black pepper for 2 to 3 minutes or until fragrant.

2 To a large bowl, add the toasted spices along with all remaining ingredients. With gloved hands or a rubber spatula, mix until thoroughly incorporated.

3 Cover with plastic wrap and refrigerate for at least 8 hours or up to 3 days.

4 To cook, form the sausage mixture into patties. Heat a large skillet over medium heat. Place the patties into the hot pan and cook for 3 to 5 minutes or until a golden brown crust forms on the bottom. Flip and repeat to cook the opposite side.

TIP   Uncooked sausage patties can be frozen between sheets of parchment paper in a zip-top freezer bag for up to 1 month before use. Cooked patties can be refrigerated for up to 3 days.

LOADED BREAKFAST BURRITO

YIELD
2 burritos

PREP TIME
5 minutes + making tortillas,
potatoes, sausage, and bacon

COOK TIME
6 minutes

I'm not a morning person, but when given something to look forward to—such as a warm breakfast burrito—the sunrise suddenly doesn't seem so bad. Even if you don't make everything homemade, this will still leave you speechless.

2 10-inch (25cm) **Flour Tortillas** (page 196)

1 cup (156g) chopped **Crispy Roasted Potatoes** (page 187)

4 patties **Italian Breakfast Sausage** (page 84), chopped

2 strips **Maple & Lemon Bacon** (page 79), chopped

½ batch **Chicken Scrambled Eggs** (page 75)

½ cup (57g) freshly grated **cheddar**

2 tbsp **vegetable oil**

1   To assemble, top each tortilla with an equal portion of potatoes, sausage, bacon, eggs, and cheese. Be sure to distribute the filling ingredients evenly so each bite has a nice mixture of everything.

2   Fold up your burritos, making sure to wrap them tightly. To wrap, fold the sides in over the filling and then bring the bottom edge of the tortilla up and over the filling, covering it completely. Snug the tortilla around the filling and then tightly roll up from the bottom. Keep it as tight as possible. (Scan the QR code for instructions.)

3   In a large pan, heat the oil over medium heat until shimmering. Add the burritos, seam side down, and cook, covered, for about 3 minutes or until the bottom of the burrito is golden brown. Flip and repeat.

TIP   You can get creative and stuff the burritos with whatever fillings you'd like. I like dipping mine in salsa and guacamole, though I don't like adding avocado inside because warm avocado is a no-no.

HOW TO FOLD
A BURRITO

SOUPS

WHILE IT HAS A TIME AND A PLACE,
SOUP LACKS TEXTURE AND EXCITEMENT.

404 ERROR

Oops, soups not found.

SAND WICHES

I WANTED TO INCLUDE THE "FLUFFERNUTTER". . .
THE PUBLISHER SAID NO.

(GO LOOK IT UP; IT'S A NEW ENGLAND CLASSIC.)

CARAMELIZED PATTY MELT

YIELD
4 sandwiches

PREP TIME
10 minutes

COOK TIME
40 minutes

This is my favorite sandwich from my college dining hall, with a sweet and chewy twist. Think grilled cheese + juicy burger + caramelized onions—all combined into a magnificent gooey mess.

¼ small **yellow onion,** finely chopped

1lb (454g) **ground beef chuck**

1 tbsp **ketchup**

2–3 dashes of **Worcestershire sauce**

½ tsp **garlic powder**

⅛ tsp **smoked paprika**

kosher salt and freshly ground **black pepper,** to taste

1 tbsp **vegetable oil**

8 slices of **sourdough** or **rye bread**

4 tbsp **mayonnaise**

1 cup (113g) freshly grated **cheddar**

½ batch **Caramelized Onions** (page 38)

1 cup (113g) freshly grated **Gruyère cheese**

1 In a medium bowl, combine the yellow onion, ground beef, ketchup, Worcestershire sauce, garlic powder, and smoked paprika. Season well with salt and pepper. Divide the mixture into 4 equal portions, and shape each portion into a wide patty.

2 In a large skillet, heat the oil over high heat. When hot, add the patties (working in batches if needed) and cook for 3 to 4 minutes until they have a dark crust on either side, flipping only once. Transfer the patties to a plate, and wipe the skillet clean with a paper towel.

3 Using a pastry brush, lightly coat one side of each slice of bread with mayonnaise, about ½ tablespoon per slice.

4 To assemble the patty melts, place 4 slices of bread on a work surface, mayonnaise side down. To each slice, add ¼ cup (28g) of cheddar, 1 patty, some caramelized onions, and ¼ cup (28g) of Gruyère. Close each sandwich with another slice of bread, mayo side up.

5 Heat the skillet over medium heat. When hot, add the patty melts, working in batches if needed. Cook for 3 minutes per side or until golden brown, pressing down firmly with a rigid spatula to achieve a golden brown crust. Serve immediately.

TIP You can use Swiss cheese for this recipe, which is somewhat traditional in a patty melt, but I'm not a big Swiss cheese fan.

BLUEBERRY BRIE GRILLED CHEESE

YIELD
4 sandwiches

PREP TIME
5 minutes

COOK TIME
20 minutes

Regular grilled cheese is delicious, but if you're craving something with a better balance of sweet and savory, try this.

8 thick slices of **sourdough bread**

4 tbsp **mayonnaise**

4 tbsp **blueberry jam** or **preserves**

6oz (170g) sliced **brie**

1 cup (140g) fresh **blueberries**

2 cups (226g) grated **sharp white cheddar**

4 tbsp **unsalted butter,** divided

1   Using a pastry brush, lightly coat one side of each slice of bread with mayonnaise, about ½ tablespoon per slice.

2   Place 4 slices of bread on a work surface, mayonnaise side down. On each of the 4 slices, spread a thin layer of blueberry jam, about 1 tablespoon per slice. Evenly distribute the brie, blueberries, and cheddar over the jam. Close each sandwich with a slice of bread, mayonnaise side up.

3   In a large nonstick pan, melt 2 tablespoons of butter over medium heat. Add 2 sandwiches and cook on one side for about 5 minutes. Use a weight, such as a small pan lid, to press down the sandwiches. Flip and cook for 5 minutes on the other side, until the exteriors of the sandwiches are browned and crisp and the cheese has melted.

4   Transfer the sandwiches to a serving platter. Repeat the cooking process for the remaining sandwiches. Serve immediately.

TIP   It is important to go low and slow, not rushing with high heat, to prevent the bread browning faster than the cheese is able to melt.

FINALLY, A GOOD BLT

YIELD
2 sandwiches

PREP TIME
7 minutes + making bacon, salt, and chicken skins

COOK TIME
5 minutes

The bacon, lettuce, and tomato sandwich has been mistreated for so many years. It lacks any sort of identity, but if each of the ingredients is treated with great care, it suddenly becomes an inexplicably good sandwich.

8 thick slices of **heirloom tomato**

Homemade Flaky Salt (page 22) and freshly ground **black pepper,** to taste

4 thick slices of **sourdough bread**

2 tbsp **mayonnaise,** plus more to taste

4 tbsp **unsalted butter**

4 strips of **Maple & Lemon Bacon** (page 79), finely chopped

4 leaves of **baby romaine lettuce**

1 batch of **Crispy Chicken Skins** (page 116)

1 Place the tomato slices in a single layer on a work surface and season with salt and pepper to taste.

2 Using a pastry brush, lightly coat one side of each slice of bread with mayonnaise, about ½ tablespoon per slice.

3 In a nonstick skillet, melt 1 tablespoon of butter over medium-high heat. Place 1 slice of bread in the skillet, mayonnaise side down, and toast for 5 to 6 minutes or until golden brown. Repeat with the remaining slices.

4 Use a pastry brush to brush the untoasted side of the bread with a thin layer of mayonnaise. Add some chopped bacon so it sticks to the mayonnaise.

5 Layer 2 leaves of baby romaine lettuce atop the bacon. Add 4 tomato slices and top the tomatoes with some crispy chicken skins. Repeat with the other sandwich. Serve immediately.

FRIED CHICKEN SANDWICH

YIELD
4 sandwiches

PREP TIME
15 minutes + making fried chicken

COOK TIME
none

For $3.99, a Popeye's classic chicken sandwich is *almost* unbeatable. But this . . . this will make you sink to the kitchen floor, gripping your sandwich in pure satisfaction.

FOR THE SANDWICH

4 pieces **Buttermilk Fried Chicken** (page 115), use skin-on thigh pieces and remove bones prior to dredging and frying

4 soft **hamburger buns,** Martin's Famous Potato Rolls recommended

8 **dill pickle slices**

FOR THE SPICY MAYO

½ cup (113g) **mayonnaise**

2 tbsp **hot sauce,** plus more to taste

1 tsp freshly squeezed **lemon juice**

¼ tsp **kosher salt**

FOR THE COLESLAW

½ cup (45g) shredded **red cabbage**

½ cup (45g) shredded **green cabbage**

¼ cup (30g) shredded **carrot**

2 tbsp **mayonnaise**

½ tsp **dill pickle juice**

¼ tsp **celery seeds**

¼ tsp **poppy seeds**

½ tsp **Brown Sugar** (page 25)

½ tsp **kosher salt**

1 For the spicy mayo, in a small bowl, combine the mayonnaise, hot sauce, lemon juice, and salt. Taste and adjust hot sauce and salt as needed. Set aside.

2 For the coleslaw, in a medium bowl, combine the red and green cabbage, carrot, mayonnaise, pickle juice, celery seeds, poppy seeds, brown sugar, and salt. Set aside.

3 To assemble, spread both sides of each bun with spicy mayo. Place two pickle slices on each bottom bun, add a piece of fried chicken, and top with a generous portion of coleslaw and the top bun. Serve immediately.

TUNA MELT

YIELD
2 sandwiches

PREP TIME
5 minutes

COOK TIME
5 minutes

When in doubt, this is my go-to lunch. Quick, filling, and exceptionally good, this open-faced tuna melt is a sandwich that never disappoints.

2 (6oz [170g]) cans of **tuna,** drained

½ tsp freshly squeezed **lemon juice**

½ tsp **lemon zest**

⅓ cup (75g) **mayonnaise**

¼ cup (36g) diced **celery**

½ tsp **smoked paprika**

kosher salt and freshly ground **black pepper,** to taste

2 large slices of **sourdough bread** or your favorite bread

1 cup (133g) grated **sharp cheddar**

2 large slices of **heirloom tomato** (optional)

1 Preheat the oven or a toaster oven to 400°F (200°C). Line a baking sheet with foil.

2 In a medium bowl, combine the tuna, lemon juice, lemon zest, mayonnaise, celery, and paprika. Season with salt and pepper to taste. Mix well with a fork to break apart and flake the tuna.

3 Top each slice of bread with an equal portion of the tuna mixture. Sprinkle an equal amount of sharp cheddar over the top of each sandwich.

4 Place the sandwiches on the prepared baking sheet. Place in the oven and cook for 3 minutes or until the cheese melts. To finish, broil on high for 1 to 2 minutes or until golden brown spots appear. (Watch carefully; the cheese can burn.)

5 Remove the sandwiches from the oven and top with sliced tomato, if using. If you opt for tomatoes, sprinkle them with salt and pepper.

TIP If you like warm tomatoes, you can add them under the cheese before melting. I like the contrast of hot, melty cheese with the cold juicy tomato, and sometimes opt for no tomato at all . . . it's all about how you're feeling that day.

GRILLED CHEESE + TOMATO SOUP

YIELD
2 sandwiches + 4 cups soup

PREP TIME
20 minutes

COOK TIME
45 minutes

Like a warm brownie with vanilla ice cream, this legendary combination is as good as it gets. Velvety smooth tomato soup and a cheesy, crusty grilled cheese is perfect for a cozy winter night or even a hot summer day (especially if you refrigerate the soup).

4 tbsp **unsalted butter,** softened, divided

½ large **yellow onion,** chopped

1 (28oz [794g]) can of **whole San Marzano tomatoes**

¾ cup (180ml) **Rotisserie Chicken Stock** (page 34)

kosher salt, to taste

4 slices of **sourdough bread**

2 tbsp **mayonnaise**

2 cups (226g) freshly grated **sharp cheddar**

1 cup (113g) freshly grated **Muenster cheese**

TIP   Use a box grater to shred your own cheese. Pre-shredded won't melt the same way.

Because of the cheese, I don't add any cream in my tomato soup, but you're welcome to add a splash of heavy cream for an extra creamy flavor.

1   In a large saucepan over medium heat, combine 2 tablespoons of butter and the onion. Sauté for 3 to 4 minutes or until onion becomes translucent. Add tomatoes and chicken stock and season with salt to taste. Bring to a simmer, then cook uncovered for 15 to 20 minutes.

2   Meanwhile, make the sandwiches. Use a pastry brush to coat one side of each slice of sourdough with ½ tablespoon of mayonnaise.

3   In a large nonstick pan, melt the remaining 2 tablespoons of butter over medium heat. Add 2 slices of bread, mayonnaise side down, and top with 1½ cups (170g) of the cheddar and all the Muenster. Add the top slices, mayonnaise side up, and cover the skillet with a lid. Cook for 3 to 5 minutes or until the bottoms become golden, then flip and repeat on the other side. Remove the sandwiches from the skillet.

4   Sprinkle the remaining cheddar in two spots, each the size of the sourdough bread footprint, in the skillet. Place each sandwich on a pile of cheese and cook until the cheese forms a golden crust on one side of the sandwich, about 5 minutes.

5   To finish the soup, carefully transfer the tomato mixture to a blender and blend on high until smooth and lighter in color— a light, velvety orange.

6   Transfer the soup into serving bowls and plate the sandwiches. Dip a sandwich into the soup to really enjoy the experience. For the best cheese pull, tear your grilled cheese with your hands instead of cutting with a knife.

CHICKEN BACON RANCH QUESADILLA

YIELD
4 quesadillas

PREP TIME
5 minutes + preparing bacon, ranch dressing, and tortillas

COOK TIME
20 to 28 minutes

If you haven't tried the combination of chicken, bacon, and ranch, now's your chance. I first discovered it at a local pizza spot back in high school, and I've loved it ever since.

1½ cups (225g) chopped **rotisserie chicken meat**

4 slices of **Maple & Lemon Bacon** (page 79), chopped

1 cup (113g) freshly grated **sharp cheddar**

1 cup (113g) freshly grated **Oaxaca cheese**

½ cup (57g) freshly grated **Monterey Jack cheese**

1 **scallion**, finely chopped

½ tsp **kosher salt**

6 tbsp **salted butter**

4 10-inch (25cm) **Flour Tortillas** (page 196)

¼ cup (60ml) **Ranch Dressing** (page 48), plus more for dipping

guacamole, to serve

salsa, to serve

1 In a medium bowl, combine the chicken, bacon, cheeses, scallion, and salt. Mix until well combined.

2 In a large nonstick skillet, melt 1½ tablespoons of butter over medium heat. Add a tortilla and spread ¼ of the filling mixture on one half of the tortilla. Drizzle some ranch dressing on top and fold the tortilla in half. Cook for 3 to 4 minutes on each side or until the cheese is melted and the tortilla becomes golden brown and crispy.

3 Remove the quesadilla from the pan and repeat step 2 to prepare the remaining quesadillas.

4 Serve immediately with ranch dressing, guacamole, and salsa.

SMASH BURGER

YIELD
4 burgers

PREP TIME
10 minutes + making sauce

COOK TIME
5 minutes

J. Kenji López-Alt has a fantastic method for making smash patties at home, and I've built upon his recipe to create a showstopping burger. You'll find that this burger is simple yet refined, with soft potato buns, crispy smash patties, melty cheese, and secret sauce.

4 soft **hamburger buns,**
Martin's Famous Potato Rolls recommended

4 tbsp **mayonnaise**

1lb (454g) **75% lean ground beef**

kosher salt and freshly ground **black pepper,** to taste

4 slices of **American cheese**

¼ cup (36g) chopped **sweet onion**

¼ cup (60ml) **Special Sauce** (page 49)

TIPS Get that pan hotter than you've ever gotten it before. If you don't commit, you'll never get a proper smash patty. The hot pan does create smoke, so I always open my doors and windows when I make these.

I like to keep my burgers simple, but feel free to add more toppings such as tomato, russet potato chips, pickles, lettuce—whatever you'd like.

1 Spread the cut sides of each bun evenly with mayonnaise. For toasted buns, heat a large nonstick skillet over medium heat and toast all 8 bun halves, working in batches, until lightly golden brown. (Sometimes I don't toast the buns and opt to let their soft and fluffy excellence speak for itself.) Set aside.

2 Place the beef in a medium bowl and "knead" it for a few seconds to mix it up. (Yes, I know; it's already ground. We're just giving it an extra bit of love.) Divide the beef into 8 balls of equal size, and weigh on a scale if you want to be extra precise. Each ball should weigh about 2 ounces (57g).

3 Heat a large stainless steel skillet over high heat for several minutes. If you have a laser temperature gun, aim for about 650°F (343°C) or hotter. If not, just leave the pan for several minutes and get it VERY hot.

4 Place 2 balls of ground beef into the dry, hot pan. Using a large, wide, rigid metal spatula and something to press it down, press on each patty firmly and evenly, moving in a circular motion to especially thin out the edges. Season with salt and pepper. Once fully pressed, leave them for about 30 seconds or until they develop a nice crust and then use your spatula to scrape up the patties and flip. Immediately add the cheese to one patty and stack the other patty atop the cheese. Repeat with the remaining patties.

5 To assemble the burgers, add the double-stacked patties to the toasted buns and top each burger with a few bits of chopped onion and special sauce. Enjoy immediately.

SMASH PATTY TECHNIQUE

CHICKEN

I ONCE RAISED A CHICKEN NAMED "NUGGET."
GUESS WHAT I EVENTUALLY TURNED HIM INTO?

FALL-APART CHICKEN CONFIT

YIELD
4 servings

PREP TIME
5 minutes + 1 hour to cool

COOK TIME
3 hours 10 minutes

The best of both worlds: crispy skin and fall-apart meat. While duck confit is one of my all-time favorites, it's far too expensive. Chicken is better suited for confit anyway, particularly given chicken meat is fattier than duck meat.

2 quarts (2 liters) **cooking oil,** plus more as needed

4 whole **chicken leg quarters,** each about 12oz (340g)

kosher salt and freshly ground **black pepper,** to taste

5 **garlic cloves**

4 sprigs of fresh **rosemary**

4 tbsp **salted butter**

1 Preheat the oven to 225°F (110°C).

2 In a large Dutch oven, heat the oil over medium heat to 200°F (95°C), about 20 minutes.

3 Season the chicken with salt and pepper. Add the chicken, garlic, and rosemary to the Dutch oven and ensure the chicken is completely covered with oil. Add more oil to cover if needed. Place a lid on the Dutch oven.

4 Place the Dutch oven in the oven and cook for 3 hours. Remove the Dutch oven from the oven and allow the chicken to cool in the oil for 1 hour.

5 In a large nonstick pan, melt 2 tablespoons of butter over medium-high heat. Carefully add 2 chicken legs skin side down and sear for 1 to 2 minutes until browned. If needed, weigh the chicken down with another pan to ensure greater surface contact with the cooking pan.

6 Carefully flip the chicken to warm up the remainder of the meat. Do this until heated just enough, about 2 minutes, such that the chicken doesn't begin to dry out. Remove from the pan and repeat steps 5 and 6 with the remaining butter and chicken legs.

7 Serve straight from the pan, skin side up, with sides of your choice, such as Velvety Mashed Potatoes (page 192).

TIP Duck fat or other poultry fat is best for making confit, but it can be hard to source and expensive. Instead, you can use any mix of vegetable oil and olive oil.

BUTTERMILK FRIED CHICKEN

YIELD
4 to 6 servings

PREP TIME
30 minutes

COOK TIME
40 minutes

I've studied fried chicken for more than a decade, and I believe it's an inherently perfect food, hitting on all the most delicious flavors and textures when properly executed.

3½lb (1.6kg) bone-in, skin-on **chicken pieces**

4 cups (960ml) **high-heat cooking oil,** for frying

kosher salt, to taste

FOR THE BRINE

2 cups (480ml) **buttermilk**

1 cup (240ml) **dill pickle juice**

1 large **egg**

3 **garlic cloves,** crushed

1 tsp **kosher salt**

FOR THE DREDGE

1½ cups (180g) **all-purpose flour**

½ cup (76g) **potato starch**

2 tbsp **cornstarch**

1 tsp **baking powder**

2 tbsp **smoked paprika**

½ tsp **cayenne pepper**

1 tbsp freshly ground **black pepper**

2 tsp **white pepper**

2 tsp **garlic powder**

2 tsp **onion powder**

2 tsp **dried oregano**

½ tsp **MSG** (optional)

1. In a large bowl, whisk together all the ingredients for the brine. Add the chicken, making sure each piece is fully submerged. Cover with plastic wrap and refrigerate for at least 30 minutes and up to 6 hours.

2. Prepare a rimmed baking sheet with a wire cooling rack. Preheat the oven to 350°F (175°C). In a large Dutch oven, begin heating the oil to 425°F (220°C) over medium-high heat. (The oil temperature will drop once you add the chicken.)

3. In a large bowl, whisk together all the ingredients for the dredge. Add 3 tablespoons of the buttermilk marinade and use your fingers to mix it around, creating small clumps.

4. Shake any excess buttermilk from each piece of chicken and coat the chicken in the dredge mixture, pressing each piece to make sure the dredge sticks. Give each piece a vigorous shake and then press once more into the dredge to fill any hidden cracks you may have missed. Shake once more and place the chicken on the prepared wire rack. As you dredge each piece of chicken, more and more clumps will form in the batter. Continue to break these apart into smaller bits with your fingers.

5. Working in batches, carefully add the chicken to the hot oil, making sure to add the pieces such that they don't stick to the bottom or one another. Adjust the heat to maintain the oil temperature at 325°F (160°C) while frying. Let the chicken fry, untouched, for 5 minutes, then rotate and fry until golden brown on all sides, about 4 to 5 minutes more.

6. Transfer the chicken to the wire rack. (The same one used previously—it's going in the oven, which will kill any bacteria.) Sprinkle immediately with salt. Place in the oven and cook for 5 minutes or until the chicken reaches an internal temperature of 165°F (74°C).

CRISPY CHICKEN SKINS

YIELD
5 to 10 pieces

PREP TIME
10 minutes

COOK TIME
15 minutes

Chicken skin is the best part of a chicken. There, I said it. In just minutes, you can crisp up the skin for the best mother-cluckin' experience you've ever had.

2 **rotisserie chickens**
seasonings of choice (optional)

1   Preheat the oven to 375°F (190°C). Prepare a rimmed baking sheet with a wire rack.

2   Remove the chicken skin. Untie any twine on the chicken legs to open up the chickens. Using your fingers, carefully separate the skin from the meat of each chicken. Try to keep each piece of skin as large and intact as possible.

3   Place the skins flat on the wire rack with ample space between them. Sprinkle with the seasonings of your choice, if desired. (Pre-seasoned rotisserie chicken may not need additional seasoning.)

4   Place the baking sheet in the oven and bake for 15 minutes or until the skins are crispy and golden brown. If any pieces get too dark, remove them from the oven.

5   Remove the rack from the oven and allow the skins to cool and become brittle before serving.

TIP   Get creative with seasonings! Za'atar is a fantastic choice. Sometimes I use smoked paprika, or you can get even bolder and more creative with something like vinegar powder.

For perfectly flat chicken skins, you can bake on a baking sheet with another rimmed baking sheet weighed down on top.

COCONUT + BUTTER CHICKEN

YIELD
6 servings

PREP TIME
1 hour

COOK TIME
35 minutes

My aunt from Lucknow, India, is an extremely talented cook. I've always loved her butter chicken, so we set out to craft an accessible version of the dish together.

2lb (907g) **boneless skinless chicken,** breasts or thighs, cut into bite-sized pieces

2 tbsp **ground coriander,** divided

1 tbsp **chili powder**

6 **garlic cloves,** minced, divided

2 tbsp finely grated **fresh ginger**

¼ cup (57g) plain **Greek yogurt**

1 tsp **kosher salt,** plus more to taste

½ cup (57g) **toasted cashews,** plus more to serve

1 tbsp **garam masala**

1 tsp **ground turmeric**

2 tsp **cumin seeds**

½ cup (116g) **tomato paste**

¼ cup (60g) **hot water**

2 tbsp **ghee**

1 large **yellow onion,** chopped

2 tbsp **granulated sugar**

freshly ground **black pepper,** to taste

4 tbsp **unsalted butter**

1 tsp **ground cayenne**

¼ tsp **ground cinnamon**

7oz (200ml) **full-fat coconut milk**

½ cup (15g) finely chopped **fresh cilantro**

cooked basmati rice, to serve

1 In a large bowl, combine the chicken, 1 tablespoon of coriander, chili powder, 3 minced garlic cloves, ginger, yogurt, and salt. Cover the bowl with plastic wrap and refrigerate for as long as time permits—at least 15 minutes but no more than 8 hours.

2 To a small bowl, add the cashews and cover with water. Soak for 1 to 2 hours. Drain and set aside.

3 In a large skillet over low heat, toast the garam masala, turmeric, cumin seeds, and the remaining 1 tablespoon of coriander for 2 to 3 minutes.

4 In a blender, combine the soaked cashews, toasted spices, tomato paste, and hot water. Blend on high until smooth. Set aside.

5 To the same skillet over medium-high heat, add the ghee, onion, and sugar. Season with salt and pepper. Cook for 3 to 5 minutes or until the onion has softened.

6 Add the marinated chicken and cook for 5 to 7 minutes or until light golden brown on all sides.

7 Add the cashew–tomato mixture, butter, cayenne, cinnamon, and remaining 3 minced garlic cloves. Cook for 5 to 8 minutes, stirring occasionally.

8 Reduce the heat to low and add the coconut milk and salt to taste. Cook until the gravy is slightly thickened.

9 Sprinkle the cilantro and extra cashews over the top. Serve with basmati rice.

DINO NUGGETS

Nobody's too old for dino nuggies. If you're embarrassed, you can swap out the dinosaur cookie cutters, but I'm convinced nuggets taste better in dinosaur form.

YIELD
40 nuggets

PREP TIME
25 minutes + 45 minutes to chill

COOK TIME
15 minutes

1 slice of **white bread**

2 tbsp **whole milk**

1 tbsp **buttermilk**

1 tsp **garlic powder**

1 tsp **onion powder**

1 tsp **kosher salt**

freshly ground **black pepper,** to taste

1lb (454g) **ground chicken**

3 large **eggs,** divided

high-heat cooking oil, for frying

1 cup **all-purpose flour**

2 tbsp **water**

1 cup **panko breadcrumbs**

1 To a large bowl, add the bread, milk, and buttermilk. Allow the bread to soak for 2 to 3 minutes. Add the garlic powder, onion powder, salt, and pepper to taste. Mix by hand. (This odd-looking paste keeps the nuggets juicy.) Add the ground chicken and 1 egg (whisked). Mix until just combined.

2 Line a rimmed baking sheet with plastic wrap. Spread the chicken mixture onto the prepared baking sheet in an even layer (it should be about ½ inch [1.25cm] thick) and freeze for about 30 minutes or until firm.

3 Remove the baking sheet from the freezer. Flip the chicken onto a dishwasher-safe cutting board and quickly cut out dinosaur shapes using 2- to 3-inch (5–7.5cm) cookie cutters. Place the nuggets back on the tray and freeze for 15 minutes.

4 In a large Dutch oven over high heat, heat at least 1 inch (2.5cm). of oil to 350°F (175°C).

5 Prepare a dredging station with 3 shallow bowls: 1 bowl of all-purpose flour, 1 bowl of the remaining 2 eggs whisked with the water, and 1 bowl of breadcrumbs.

6 Remove the nuggets from the freezer. Dredge the dino shapes in the flour, then the egg, and finally the breadcrumbs.

7 Working in batches, add the nuggets to the hot oil and fry for about 5 minutes or until golden brown. Transfer the nuggets to a wire rack to cool slightly before serving.

ROTISSERIE CHICKEN SALAD

YIELD
4 servings

PREP TIME
15 minutes

COOK TIME
none

I define a good "leftover" dish as one that doesn't feel like leftovers. This. Is. It.

2 cups (300g) chopped **rotisserie chicken**

1½ **celery stalks,** diced

⅓ cup (47g) diced **red onion**

½ cup (112g) **mayonnaise**

¼ cup (57g) **sour cream** or **crème fraîche**

1 tsp chopped **fresh dill**

1 tsp **Brown Sugar** (page 25)

juice and zest of 1 **lemon,** divided

kosher salt and freshly ground **black pepper,** to taste

1 In a large serving bowl, combine the chicken, celery, onion, mayonnaise, sour cream, dill, sugar, and 1 teaspoon of lemon juice. Mix well to ensure everything has been fully incorporated.

2 Season with salt and pepper to taste. Using a Microplane grater, grate some lemon zest over the top before serving.

TIP Want your guests to go crazy? Serve spoonfuls of this chicken salad atop Crispy Chicken Skins (page 116) as an appetizer. They're bite-sized and delectable.

BUFFALO CHICKEN EGG ROLLS

YIELD
10 egg rolls

PREP TIME
25 minutes + making ranch
and buffalo sauce

COOK TIME
8 to 10 minutes

This is a food where you make it, take a bite, and then go, *Oh, that's good.* I don't know what else to say about it. It's delicious.

½ cup (120g) **Ranch Dressing** (page 48)

3 tbsp **blue cheese crumbles** (optional)

1½ cups (224g) shredded **rotisserie chicken**

2 cups (226g) shredded **mozzarella**

4oz (113g) **cream cheese,** softened

¼ cup (60ml) **Buffalo Sauce** (page 50)

4 **scallions,** thinly sliced

⅓ cup (47g) diced **celery**

kosher salt and freshly ground **black pepper,** to taste

10 square **egg roll wrappers**

1 cup **high-heat cooking oil,** for frying

1. In a small bowl, combine the ranch dressing and blue cheese crumbles (if using). Refrigerate until ready to serve.

2. In a medium bowl, combine the chicken, mozzarella, cream cheese, buffalo sauce, scallions, and celery. Season with salt and pepper to taste.

3. Place an egg roll wrapper on a clean work surface in a diamond orientation. Using the tip of your finger, lightly moisten the edges of the wrapper with water.

4. Place a log-shaped portion (about 4 tablespoons) of the filling in the wrapper. Fold the right side of the wrapper over the filling, tucking it tightly around. Then fold down the top corner of the wrapper and fold up the bottom corner so the points overlap in the middle. Finally, roll the wrapper to the left to seal it. Repeat with the remaining wrappers and filling.

5. In a Dutch oven, heat the oil over medium-high heat until the oil starts to bubble. To test if the oil is hot enough, place an unfilled egg roll wrapper in the oil. If it immediately begins to puff up and crisp, the oil is ready.

6. When the oil is hot, add half the egg rolls and fry for about 2 minutes per side or until golden brown. Repeat with the remaining egg rolls.

7. Using a slotted spoon, transfer the egg rolls to a plate lined with paper towels. Allow them to cool slightly. (I've burned the roof of my mouth several times with these!)

8. Transfer the egg rolls to a serving dish. Serve with the ranch and blue cheese dressing.

HOW TO ROLL
AN EGG ROLL

THAI CHICKEN NOODLE SOUP

YIELD
5 servings

PREP TIME
10 minutes

COOK TIME
5 minutes

This is one of the few soups in my book for a reason: It deserves to be here. Every recipe earned its place—and this is a comforting, complex soup that'll remind you why you love food.

1 tbsp **coconut oil**

½ **yellow onion**, thinly sliced

1 tbsp **coconut sugar** or **Brown Sugar** (page 25)

1–2 tsp **kosher salt**

2 **garlic cloves**, minced

2 tbsp **Thai green curry paste**

6 cups **Rotisserie Chicken Stock** (page 34)

1 (13.5oz [398ml]) can of **coconut milk**

1 tbsp **fish sauce**

4oz (113g) **thin rice noodles**

2 **red bell peppers**, thinly sliced

1 **scallion**, thinly sliced

1lb (454g) shredded **rotisserie chicken meat**

2 tbsp freshly squeezed **lime juice**, plus more to taste

1 cup (25g) chopped **fresh cilantro**, plus more to garnish

lime wedges, to garnish

½ cup crushed **peanuts** (optional), to garnish

chili oil (optional), to garnish

1 In a large pot, heat the coconut oil over medium heat. Add the onion and coconut sugar. Cook the onion for about 5 minutes or until softened, stirring often. Add the salt.

2 Add the garlic and curry paste. Cook for 1 to 2 minutes.

3 Add the chicken stock, coconut milk, and fish sauce. Cover the pot and increase the heat to bring the mixture to a boil.

4 Add the rice noodles, breaking them up a bit as you drop them in. Add the bell peppers, scallion, and chicken. Cook for 3 minutes.

5 Stir in the lime juice and cilantro. Taste and adjust the seasoning as needed. Remove the pot from the heat.

6 Before serving, garnish each bowl with cilantro, a lime wedge, peanuts (if using), and chili oil (if using).

TIP Please make your own chicken stock (or buy a high-quality one) for this dish! You'll already have a rotisserie chicken carcass ready to go. For boosted cilantro flavor, add chopped cilantro stems to your chicken stock as it simmers.

HOW TO SHRED CHICKEN

MEAT

CALLING ALL CARNIVORES. WHO'S READY
FOR THE MEAT SWEATS?

CAST-IRON RIBEYE

YIELD
2 servings

PREP TIME
2 minutes + 10 minutes to rest

COOK TIME
15 minutes

I often joke that you're not properly searing your steak until you've set off the fire alarm. The primary difference between a professional chef and a home cook when it comes to achieving a nice crust? Heat. Crank it up!

2 bone-in **rib-eye steaks,** each about 1lb (454g), at room temperature

kosher salt and freshly ground **black pepper,** to taste

high-heat cooking oil, for searing

4 tbsp **unsalted butter**

2 sprigs of **fresh rosemary**

4 **garlic cloves,** crushed

1   Place a wire rack on a rimmed baking sheet. Pat the steaks dry and generously season on all sides with salt and pepper.

2   To a large cast-iron skillet over high heat, add oil to coat the bottom. I like to add enough oil to go up the side of the steak by a few millimeters, giving me a larger and more defined crust. Let the oil heat for a few minutes.

3   When the oil begins to smoke, add a steak to the skillet, pressing down for a moment to maximize surface contact. Cook one steak at a time so you don't overcrowd the pan. DO NOT TOUCH THE STEAK. Leave it alone to allow the crust to form.

4   After about 2 minutes, flip the steak. Cook for the same amount of time on the opposite side, allowing it to cook evenly and achieve a crust.

5   Using tongs, lift the steak and sear the edges, gently rolling it around in the skillet. While holding the steak against the skillet, carefully pour out the oil. Return the skillet to the heat and add 2 tablespoons of butter. When the butter has melted, add 1 sprig of rosemary and 2 garlic cloves.

6   Using a large spoon, baste the steak with butter or flip the steak a few more times to coat with the flavors. Remove the steak from the pan just before the internal temperature reaches your desired doneness: 135°F (55°C) for medium-rare or 145°F (60°C) for medium. Transfer the steak to a wire rack to rest for 5 to 7 minutes, placing the rosemary and garlic on top. (Remember, the steak will continue to cook once off the heat.) Wipe the pan clean and repeat to cook the remaining steak.

7   After resting, slice the steaks—the moment of truth, I call it—and enjoy! Serve with Velvety Mashed Potatoes (page 192) and Persian Street Corn (page 213).

FALL-APART OVEN RIBS

YIELD
4 servings

PREP TIME
15 minutes + 30 minutes to rest

COOK TIME
1 hour 40 minutes + 15 minutes to cool

I had the best pork ribs of my life from my friend Todd, the pitmaster and mastermind behind one of the best BBQ joints in Texas. Together, we created this recipe to make great ribs more accessible—not everybody has a giant smoker lying around.

2 racks of **pork baby back ribs,** each about 3½lb (1.6kg)

3 tbsp **kosher salt**

3 tbsp freshly ground **black pepper**

1 tbsp **garlic powder**

1 tbsp **onion powder**

1 tbsp **paprika**

½ tsp **chili powder**

2 tbsp **granulated sugar**

2 tbsp **Brown Sugar** (page 25)

1 cup (288g) **Barbecue Sauce** (page 51), plus more to serve

1 Remove the membrane from the ribs. (Many people forget this step, but it's a must for fall-off-the-bone ribs. Scan the QR code for instructions.) Place the ribs in a large container.

2 In a small bowl, combine the salt, pepper, garlic powder, onion powder, paprika, chili powder, and sugars. Rub the ribs with this mixture, coating them fully. Allow the rub to penetrate the meat for at least 30 minutes or up to overnight. (If marinating for more than 30 minutes, cover with plastic wrap and refrigerate.)

3 Position an oven rack in the upper-middle level. Preheat the broiler to high. Line a rimmed baking sheet with aluminum foil and a wire rack. Transfer the ribs to the prepared baking sheet and place in the oven. Broil for 10 minutes or until the sugars begin to caramelize and form a crust on the ribs.

4 Remove the ribs from the oven and preheat the oven to 350°F (175°C). Wrap the ribs tightly in foil. Place the wrapped ribs on a baking sheet. Place in the oven and cook for 90 minutes.

5 Remove the ribs from the oven and let cool for 15 minutes, still wrapped.

6 Unwrap the ribs and drizzle barbecue sauce over the top. Serve the ribs with more sauce on the side.

TIP You can also grill these ribs instead of broiling in step 3. Preheat the grill to high and cook the ribs for 3 to 5 minutes per side just to char the ribs and create some color while cooking the surface. Finish in the oven as directed.

↑
HOW TO REMOVE THE RIB MEMBRANE

MINTY LAMB LOLLIPOPS

YIELD
4 servings

PREP TIME
10 minutes

COOK TIME
15 minutes

Lamb was a special treat in my family, and my favorite part of the meal was always the bright green, spearmint-flavored jelly served alongside it. I find this dish pairs quite well with Papa's Crispy Rice (page 188).

12 **lollipop lamb chops,** each about 3½oz (100g)

kosher salt and freshly ground **black pepper,** to taste

3 tbsp **high-heat cooking oil,** plus more if needed

3 tbsp **Simple Homemade Butter** (page 30), melted

¼ cup (8g) **fresh mint leaves,** chiffonade

3 tbsp **mint jelly,** plus more for serving

1 **lemon,** to grate for zest

1 Season each lamb chop on all sides with salt and pepper.

2 In a large cast-iron skillet, heat the oil over medium-high heat until it shimmers.

3 Cook the lamb chops in several batches to avoid crowding the pan. If your lamb chops have a fat cap, start by placing them in the skillet fat side down for 1 to 2 minutes to render the fat.

4 When the fat cap has rendered, evenly space the lamb chops in the skillet and cook for about 3 minutes per side. (Do not move them around as they cook.) Transfer to a serving platter to rest and repeat with the remaining lamb chops, adding more oil if needed.

5 In a small bowl, combine the butter, fresh mint, and mint jelly. Stir until well combined.

6 Using a brush, coat each lamb chop with the mint–butter mixture. Grate lemon zest over the top and enjoy immediately.

TIP Mint jelly is one of the few ingredients where I feel that the cheaper it is, the better it tastes. Get that unhealthy, high-fructose, bright-spearmint-green jelly. (Sorry, Mom.) Live a little.

COZY BEEF CHILI

YIELD
6 servings

PREP TIME
5 minutes

COOK TIME
55 minutes

A chili craving should only be satisfied one way: Make it at home. I've had the pleasure of making chili alongside Brian Baumgartner (Kevin Malone from *The Office*) and I've implemented a few of his tricks here!

4 tbsp **extra-virgin olive oil**

1 large **yellow onion,** diced

1 **red bell pepper,** diced

1 tbsp **Brown Sugar** (page 25)

3 **garlic cloves,** minced

2lb (907g) **80% lean ground beef**

2 tbsp **chili powder**

1½ tsp **smoked paprika**

½ tsp **ground cumin**

1 tsp **onion powder**

½ tsp **kosher salt**

¾ tsp **freshly ground black pepper**

⅛ tsp **ground cayenne**

½ cup (120ml) **dry white wine**

1½ cups (360ml) **beef stock** or **Rotisserie Chicken Stock** (page 34)

1 (28oz [794g]) can of **crushed San Marzano tomatoes**

1 (14.5oz [411g]) can of **fire-roasted diced tomatoes**

1 (16oz [454g]) can of **red kidney beans,** rinsed and drained

1 (16oz [454g]) can of **pinto beans,** rinsed and drained

2 tbsp **Worcestershire sauce**

TO SERVE (OPTIONAL)
sour cream
shredded **yellow cheddar**
shredded **white cheddar**
sliced **scallions**
lime wedges

1 In a large Dutch oven, heat the olive oil over medium heat until it shimmers. Add the onion, bell pepper, and brown sugar. Cook for 3 to 5 minutes, stirring frequently until the onion and pepper have softened. Add the garlic and sauté for 30 to 45 seconds, stirring constantly.

2 Add the ground beef, stirring and breaking it apart until lightly browned and crumbly, about 4 to 5 minutes.

3 Add the chili powder, paprika, cumin, onion powder, salt, pepper, and cayenne. Stir to combine. Add the wine, stock, tomatoes, kidney beans, pinto beans, and Worcestershire sauce. Bring to a boil, then reduce the heat to a simmer and cook uncovered for 30 to 45 minutes, stirring occasionally. Adjust the heat as necessary to reach the desired consistency.

4 Remove the Dutch oven from the heat. Serve the chili with sour cream, yellow and white cheddar cheese, scallions, and lime wedges or your favorite toppings.

TIPS Substitute plant-based meat to make this vegetarian, and use nondairy accompaniments to make it vegan.

For more heat, increase the ground cayenne or add chopped jalapeños.

CHILI WITH BRIAN BAUMGARTNER

GARLIC BUTTER STEAK TIPS

YIELD
3 servings

PREP TIME
2 minutes

COOK TIME
14 minutes

Steak tips are a distinctly New England—and, more specifically, Boston—dish. Bite-sized steak tossed in a delicious white wine garlic butter—what's not to love?

1½lb (680g) **top sirloin steak,** cubed

kosher salt and freshly ground **black pepper**

2 tbsp **vegetable oil**

4 **garlic cloves,** minced

⅓ cup (80ml) **dry white wine**

2 tbsp **unsalted butter**

chopped **flat-leaf parsley,** to garnish

1 Generously season the steak all over with salt and pepper. In a large cast-iron skillet, heat the oil over high heat. When the oil begins to shimmer, add half the steak to the skillet, making sure there's space between each piece. Cook without touching or moving anything for about 1 minute or until the steak cubes are nicely browned on one side. Stir the cubes, then flip them and cook for 1 minute more. Transfer to a medium bowl. Repeat with the remaining steak cubes and set aside.

2 Reduce the heat to medium and add the garlic. Sauté for about 30 seconds or until lightly golden brown, stirring often. Add the wine and use a wooden spatula to scrape the bottom of the pan, loosening all the flavorful bits. Cook for about 3 minutes to cook off the alcohol and thicken the sauce slightly.

3 Reduce the heat to medium-low and add the butter. Once the butter has melted, return all the steak cubes to the skillet. Toss to lightly coat.

4 Transfer everything to a serving dish and sprinkle with parsley. Serve the steak tips and their delicious juices with rice or skewer on toothpicks to serve as an appetizer.

TIP Instead of top sirloin, try using New York strip steak, tenderloin, ribeye, or really any cut of steak you like.

SHEPHERD'S PIE

YIELD
10 to 12 servings

PREP TIME
10 minutes + making
the mashed potatoes

COOK TIME
55 minutes

This comforting, humble, and undeniably delicious casserole was one of my favorite dishes as a kid. Although it's commonly made with beef, I prefer to use the traditional ground lamb.

2 tbsp **unsalted butter**

1 large **yellow onion,** diced

2 medium **carrots,** diced

2lb (907g) **ground lamb**

½ tsp **kosher salt**

½ tsp freshly ground **black pepper**

5 tbsp **all-purpose flour**

1 tbsp **tomato paste**

¼ cup (60ml) **heavy cream**

1¾ cups (420ml) **low-sodium chicken broth**

¾ cup (180ml) **light beer**

2 tbsp **soy sauce**

2 tsp minced **fresh thyme**

1 cup (140g) **frozen peas**

4 cups (840g) **Velvety Mashed Potatoes** (page 192)

1 **egg yolk**

1 tbsp **water**

freshly grated **Parmesan cheese** (optional)

1 Preheat the oven to 400°F (200°C).

2 In a large skillet, melt the butter over medium heat until foamy. Add the onion and carrot. Cook for 7 minutes or until al dente. Add the lamb, salt, and pepper. Cook for 7 to 8 minutes, stirring frequently until the meat is browned.

3 Pour off as much rendered fat as possible. Stir in the flour and tomato paste. Cook, stirring frequently, for about 1 minute or until the tomato paste is well combined. Stir in the cream and cook for about 1 minute. Stir in the chicken broth, beer, soy sauce, and thyme. Simmer for 10 to 15 minutes.

4 Remove the skillet from the heat and stir in the peas. Transfer the filling to a large cast-iron skillet or a 9 × 13-inch (23 × 33cm) glass or ceramic baking dish. Using a rubber spatula, spread the mashed potatoes evenly over the filling.

5 In a small bowl, whisk the egg yolk and water to make an egg wash. Brush the mashed potatoes with the egg wash and drag a fork across the top to create ridges. If desired, use a Microplane grater to lightly grate some Parmesan cheese over the top.

6 Place in the oven and bake for about 20 minutes or until the filling is bubbling around the edges. Turn on the broiler and broil for 3 to 5 minutes or until the topping is golden brown.

7 Remove from the oven and allow to cool slightly before serving.

SWEDISH MEATBALLS

YIELD
4 servings

PREP TIME
10 minutes

COOK TIME
25 minutes

You don't need to go to a furniture store to get delicious meatballs. This recipe pairs incredibly well with mashed potatoes and jam, egg noodles, or rice.

½lb (227g) **80% lean ground beef**

½lb (227g) **ground pork**

¼ cup (13g) **panko breadcrumbs**

¼ cup (36g) finely chopped **yellow onion**

1 large **egg**

½ tsp **garlic powder**

½ tsp **kosher salt**

½ tsp freshly ground **black pepper**

¼ tsp **ground allspice**

¼ tsp **ground nutmeg**

2 tbsp + ⅓ cup (75g) **unsalted butter,** divided

⅓ cup (40g) **all-purpose flour**

1½ cups (360ml) **Rotisserie Chicken Stock** (page 34)

⅓ cup (80ml) **heavy cream**

2 tsp **soy sauce**

2 tsp **Worcestershire sauce**

½ tsp **Dijon mustard**

chopped **fresh parsley,** to garnish

1 In a medium bowl, combine the beef, pork, breadcrumbs, onion, egg, garlic powder, salt, pepper, allspice, and nutmeg. Mix by hand until well combined.

2 With lightly oiled hands, form the meat mixture into 16 balls of equal size.

3 In a large skillet, melt 2 tablespoons of butter over medium-high heat. Add the meatballs and cook until they develop a golden crust on all sides, about 4 to 5 minutes per side. Transfer to a plate, cover with foil, and set aside.

4 In the same skillet, melt the remaining ⅓ cup (75g) of butter over medium heat. When the butter has melted, whisk in the flour and cook for 5 to 7 minutes or until it turns a deep golden brown. Gradually stir in the chicken stock and increase the heat to medium-high, stirring until the sauce becomes thickened to your liking.

5 Add the heavy cream, soy sauce, Worcestershire sauce, and mustard. Taste and season with salt and pepper as needed. Add the meatballs to the skillet and simmer over low heat for 2 to 3 minutes or until the sauce has reached a thick, velvety consistency.

6 Transfer to a serving dish and garnish with chopped parsley.

TIP You can omit the pork and make all-beef meatballs using 1 pound (454g) of ground beef, if desired.

PORK BELLY KHAO SOI

YIELD
6 servings

PREP TIME
10 minutes + 6 hours to marinate

COOK TIME
1 hour 10 minutes

A friend from Thailand sat me down for my first-ever bowl of *khao soi* several years ago. After taking the first bite, I paused and slowly looked up at him as if to ask, *What is this and why didn't I know about it sooner?* It's a flavor-packed coconut curry noodle dish, in this case topped with crispy pork belly. It is simply unbelievable.

1lb (454g) **pork belly,** sliced into strips 1 inch (2.5cm) wide and ¼ inch (6mm) thick

4 cups (960ml) **water**

¼ cup (32g) + 1½ tbsp **kosher salt,** divided

¼ cup (53g) **Brown Sugar** (page 25)

1 tbsp **whole peppercorns**

3 **bay leaves**

3 **garlic cloves,** crushed

high-heat cooking oil, for frying

1lb (454g) **fresh egg noodles,** divided

5 tbsp **red curry paste**

1 tbsp **mild Thai curry powder**

½ tsp **turmeric powder**

¼ cup (60ml) **fish sauce**

2 tbsp **soy sauce**

3oz (85g) **palm** or **coconut sugar**

2 cups (480ml) **Rotisserie Chicken Stock** (page 34)

3 cups (720ml) **unsweetened coconut milk**

TO SERVE

2 tbsp **unsweetened coconut cream,** warmed

1 cup (130g) **sauerkraut**

sliced **scallions,** cut on a bias

a few sprigs of **fresh cilantro**

6 **lime wedges**

1. To a large pot, add the pork belly, water, ¼ cup (32g) salt, brown sugar, peppercorns, bay leaves, and garlic. Bring to a boil over high heat. When boiling, reduce the heat to medium, partially cover, and simmer for 30 minutes or until the meat is tender.

2. Remove the pork belly (discard the cooking liquid) and pat dry with paper towels. Transfer to a baking sheet lined with a wire rack and rub all over with 1 tablespoon of salt. Place in the refrigerator, uncovered, for at least 6 hours or overnight.

3. Cut the pork belly strips into 1-inch (2.5cm) squares. To a large Dutch oven, add 4 inches (10cm) of oil and heat to 375°F (190°C). Working in batches, fry the pork until golden brown and crispy, about 5 to 7 minutes per batch. Transfer to a plate lined with a paper towel. Maintain the oil temperature and add 4 ounces (113g) of the noodles. Fry until crispy and golden brown, about 2 minutes. Transfer to a plate lined with a paper towel and set aside.

4. In a large pot, heat 2 tablespoons of oil over medium-low heat until it shimmers. Add the curry paste, curry powder, and turmeric. Cook, stirring often, for 8 minutes. Stir in the fish sauce, soy sauce, palm sugar, and the remaining ½ tablespoon of salt. Cook for 2 minutes. Add the stock and coconut milk, and increase the heat to medium-high. Bring the mixture to a simmer, then lower the heat to maintain the simmer and cook, uncovered, while you prepare the noodles.

5. Bring a large pot of water to a boil and add the remaining 12 ounces (340g) of noodles. Cook according to the package instructions until tender. Drain.

6. To serve, divide the cooked noodles evenly among four shallow bowls. To each bowl, add a ladle of curry and a drizzle of coconut cream. Top with fried pork belly, fried noodles, sauerkraut, scallions, and cilantro. Serve with lime wedges.

SEAFOOD

I'M ALWAYS ON A SEAFOOD DIET. I SEE FOOD, AND I EAT IT.

BROWNED BUTTER LOBSTER ROLL

YIELD
4 lobster rolls

PREP TIME
15 minutes

COOK TIME
10 minutes

As a New Englander with a recreational lobster fishing license that I use every summer, I've spent more than a decade perfecting this lobster roll. It boasts a playful balance of hot and cold, and it ultimately highlights the true star: fresh, delicious lobster.

4 tbsp **unsalted butter,** softened, divided

2 tbsp **dry milk powder**

½ tsp freshly squeezed **lemon juice**

½ tsp **lemon zest**

½ cup (112g) **mayonnaise**

1lb (454g) cooked **lobster meat,** cut into medium chunks

Homemade Flaky Salt (page 22), to taste

4 **split-top brioche hot dog buns**

TO GARNISH
fresh **fennel fronds**
fresh **dill fronds**
thinly sliced **fresh chives**

1. In a medium skillet, melt 2 tablespoons of butter over medium heat. When the butter has melted, whisk in the milk powder and cook until the solids begin to brown, about 3 minutes. (The milk solids will continue to cook off of the heat, so stop cooking just as they begin to brown.)

2. Transfer the butter mixture to a medium bowl. Stir in the lemon juice and lemon zest. Allow the mixture to cool.

3. Stir in the mayonnaise. Add the lobster meat and season with salt to taste. Gently mix to combine. Set aside.

4. Using a bread knife, slice a thin layer of the brown crust from the long sides of each bun, exposing the light bread beneath. Spread the exposed bread with the remaining 2 tablespoons of butter, about ½ tablespoon per bun.

5. In a large skillet over medium heat, toast the sides of the buns for 2 to 3 minutes per side or until a golden brown crust forms.

6. Transfer the buns to a serving platter and stuff each bun with an equal portion of the lobster filling. Sprinkle with the fennel fronds, dill, and chives before serving.

HOW TO COOK A LOBSTER AND REMOVE LOBSTER MEAT

SCALLOPED SCALLOPS

YIELD
2 to 4 servings

PREP TIME
15 minutes

COOK TIME
12 to 15 minutes

My grandmother Helga was unquestionably the greatest cook in our family. After searching through her entire wooden recipe box (that's when you know somebody is legit), this was my favorite recipe by far. Refined and truly mind-blowing.

½ cup (113g) **unsalted butter,** melted, plus more for greasing

1lb (454g) **large sea scallops**

1 cup (112g) crushed **Ritz crackers**

½ cup (25g) **panko breadcrumbs**

⅔ cup (160ml) **heavy cream**

kosher salt and freshly ground **black pepper,** to taste

1 **lemon,** to grate for zest

chopped **fresh chives,** to garnish

chopped **fresh parsley,** to garnish

1   Preheat the oven to 400°F (200°C). Grease a small baking dish, about 6 × 8 inches (15 × 20cm), with butter.

2   Thinly slice the scallops horizontally into rounds (2 to 3 slices per scallop) and set aside.

3   In a small bowl, combine the melted butter, crackers, and breadcrumbs. Stir until a crumbly mixture forms.

4   In the buttered dish, add a layer of the cracker mixture, then cover that with some scallop slices and about ⅓ of the heavy cream. Season with salt and pepper to taste. Using a Microplane grater, zest a little of the lemon over the top.

5   Repeat step 4 two more times, finishing with a final layer of the cracker mixture.

6   Bake for 12 to 15 minutes or until golden brown. Remove the dish from the oven, and sprinkle the chives and parsley over the top before serving.

TIP   When shopping for scallops, be picky. Look for dry-packed scallops (rather than wet-packed scallops). Dry scallops taste and sear better, not to mention they save you money on added water weight.

FISH 'N' CHIPS
WITH CURRIED AIOLI

My grandpa's go-to restaurant order was fish and chips. After testing countless iterations, this is the best fried fish I've ever had, combined with a UK chip shop–style curry sauce. This one's for you, Grandpa.

YIELD
3 to 4 servings

PREP TIME
10 minutes

COOK TIME
20 minutes

8 cups (1.9 liters) **high-heat cooking oil,** for frying

2lb (907g) skinless **cod,** about 1 inch (2.5cm) thick

kosher salt and freshly ground **black pepper,** to taste

½ cup (60g) **all-purpose flour**

french fries, to serve

lemon wedges, to serve

FOR THE BATTER

⅓ cup (40g) **all-purpose flour**

⅓ cup (50g) **potato starch**

⅓ cup (37g) **cornstarch**

½ tsp **baking powder**

¾ cup (180ml) **light beer** or **sparkling water**

FOR THE CURRIED AOLI

1½ cups (336g) **mayonnaise**

2 tsp **curry powder**

¼ tsp **garlic powder**

¼ tsp **onion powder**

½ tsp **ground ginger**

2 tbsp **malt vinegar**

sea salt, to taste

½ tsp **lemon zest**

1   To make the curried aioli, combine all the ingredients in a medium bowl. Cover and refrigerate until ready to serve.

2   To make the batter, in a large bowl, whisk together the flour, potato starch, cornstarch, and baking powder. Add the beer and whisk until smooth. Cover and refrigerate until ready to use.

3   In a large Dutch oven, heat the oil to 375°F (190°C) over medium heat.

4   Cut the cod into 8 portions, each about 4 ounces (113g). Pat dry with paper towels, and season well with salt and pepper.

5   Spread the flour in a shallow bowl and remove the batter from the fridge. Lightly dredge each piece of fish in the flour, shaking to remove excess. Quickly dip the fish in the batter to coat and immediately move to the next step.

6   Add the fish into the oil one piece at a time to ensure they don't stick to the bottom or each other. Do not add more than four pieces at a time. Cook each piece for 4 to 5 minutes per side until golden brown.

7   Remove the fish from the oil and transfer them to a wire cooling rack. Lightly sprinkle salt over the top. Serve the fish with french fries, the curried aioli, and lemon wedges for squeezing.

FRIED CALAMARI
WITH SQUID INK AIOLI

YIELD
2 to 3 servings

PREP TIME
15 minutes

COOK TIME
10 minutes

I have fond childhood memories of catching squid late at night, using flashlights to attract them to the surface of the ocean and getting sprayed with their jet-black ink while pulling them onto land. The beautiful ink is too iconic not to include on the plate.

high-heat cooking oil, for frying

¾ cup (180ml) **whole milk**

1 tbsp **sea salt,** plus more to finish

1lb (454g) **squid,** cut into ¾-inch (2cm) sections

¾ cup (80g) sliced **pickled peppers** (banana or hot cherry peppers recommended)

1 cup (120g) **all-purpose flour**

½ cup (76g) **potato starch**

¼ cup (35g) **cornmeal**

1 tbsp **baking powder**

freshly ground **black pepper,** to taste

lemon wedges, to serve

FOR THE AIOLI

½ cup (112g) **mayonnaise**

1 tsp **squid ink** or **charcoal powder** (optional)

2 tsp freshly squeezed **lemon juice**

1–2 **garlic cloves,** finely minced

pinch of **ground cayenne**

1. In a large Dutch oven, heat 4 inches (10cm) of oil to 350°F (175°C) over high heat.

2. In a large bowl, combine the milk and salt. Add the squid and peppers, and soak for 5 minutes.

3. In a medium bowl, whisk together the flour, potato starch, cornmeal, and baking powder.

4. Remove the squid and peppers from the milk mixture. Shake off any excess liquid and dredge the squid and peppers in the flour mixture. After dredging, let them sit for a few minutes before frying. (This helps prevent the coating from flaking off.)

5. Slowly add the squid and peppers to the hot oil and fry for about 3 minutes or until golden brown. Remove the squid and peppers with a slotted spoon and place them on a wire rack covered with paper towels. Immediately sprinkle with sea salt and pepper.

6. To make the aioli, in a small bowl, stir together all the ingredients until well combined.

7. Transfer the squid and peppers to a serving plate. Garnish with the lemon wedges for squeezing and serve with the squid ink aioli for dipping.

AIR FRYER SALMON

YIELD
2 servings

PREP TIME
3 minutes

COOK TIME
8 to 12 minutes

I'll admit it: I used to hate air fryers. There's been too much hype, despite the fact that it's not that novel of an idea. (It's just a mini convection oven.) But after creating this no-fail salmon recipe, I think I might be in love.

2 skin-on **salmon fillets**, each about 8oz (227g)

sea salt and freshly ground **black pepper,** to taste

2 tbsp **mayonnaise**

freshly grated **Parmesan cheese** (optional)

1   Preheat the air fryer to 400°F (200°C).

2   Rub each fillet with salt and pepper and then fully coat each fillet in mayonnaise. Grate some Parmesan cheese over the top, if using.

3   Place the salmon in the air fryer basket skin side down and cook for 8 to 12 minutes depending on the thickness of the fillets. Thicker fillets will require a longer cook time.

4   Using a fork, check for doneness after 8 minutes of cooking and do not overcook. The salmon should be flaky but still extremely juicy, with no white substance (albumin—the mark of overcooked salmon) coming from the sides of the fish.

TIPS   Every air fryer is different. Watch carefully, and remove your salmon when it's just barely flaky all the way through.

Serve the salmon with rice cooked in coconut milk and some lime zest to taste. Delicious!

TUNA CRISPY RICE

YIELD
15 pieces

PREP TIME
25 minutes

COOK TIME
50 minutes

This crispy, chewy bite has become a favorite in sushi restaurants everywhere. My version features a creamy, tangy dressing with hints of honey and optional truffle.

1lb (454g) **sushi-grade tuna,** ½-inch (1.25cm) dice

¼ cup (56g) **mayonnaise**

1 tbsp **soy sauce**

1 tbsp **chili crisp**

2 tsp **sesame oil,** divided

1 tsp **lime zest**

truffle salt, to taste

sriracha (optional), to taste

2 cups (400g) **sushi rice**

3 cups (720ml) **water**

⅓ cup (80ml) **rice vinegar**

½ cup (120ml) + 4 tbsp **high-heat cooking oil,** divided

¼ cup (50g) **granulated sugar**

1 tsp **kosher salt**

1 **avocado** (optional), ½-inch (1.25cm) dice

TO GARNISH

2 tbsp toasted **sesame seeds**

⅓ cup (20g) thinly sliced **scallions**

2 tbsp **truffle oil**

2 tbsp **honey** or **hot honey**

TIP If you're left with extra rice and tuna, add some diced cucumber, diced mango, or whatever else you'd like to make a poke bowl the next day!

1 In a medium bowl, combine the tuna, mayonnaise, soy sauce, chili crisp, 1 teaspoon of sesame oil, and lime zest. Add the truffle salt and sriracha (if using) to taste. Cover and refrigerate the mixture until ready to assemble.

2 In a fine-mesh strainer, rinse the rice under cold water until the water runs clear. In a medium saucepan, combine the rice and water, and bring to a boil over medium-high heat. Once boiling, reduce the heat to low and cover with a lid. Cook for 20 minutes, covered, or until the rice is tender. Using a rubber spatula, transfer the cooked rice to a large bowl.

3 In a medium saucepan, combine the rice vinegar, ½ cup (120ml) of oil, sugar, and kosher salt. Place over medium heat for 3 to 4 minutes, stirring frequently, until the sugar dissolves. Remove the pan from the heat and allow the mixture to cool slightly. Using a rubber spatula, stir the vinegar mixture into the cooked rice, folding it in gently until all the liquid has been absorbed.

4 Place a piece of parchment paper on a cutting board. Place a small ring mold on the parchment paper and press the rice into the mold to create a disk that's about 1½ inches (3.75cm) in diameter and ½ inch (1.25cm) thick. Repeat until all the rice has been formed into patties. (You will make about 15 patties.)

5 In a large nonstick skillet, heat 2 tablespoons of oil over high heat. When hot, add the rice patties, working in batches to avoid crowding the pan. Cook for 4 minutes or until a golden brown crust forms, then flip. Add the remaining 2 tablespoons of oil to the pan and cook for 4 minutes more. Transfer the patties to a wire rack and repeat until all the patties have been fried.

6 If using avocado, gently mix it into the tuna mixture. Immediately begin spooning the tuna mixture evenly over the patties. Top each one with sesame seeds, scallions, truffle oil, and honey.

SHRIMP CEVICHE

Peruvian cuisine is as refreshing as it is delicious. This recipe, which "cooks" shrimp in a flavorful lemon-lime juice mixture, is a fantastic introduction to the world of ceviche and doesn't carry any sort of fishy flavor that some people tend to dislike.

YIELD
10 to 12 servings

PREP TIME
10 minutes + 30 minutes to marinate

COOK TIME
1 minute

1lb (454g) **raw medium shrimp,** deveined and tails removed

juice of 3 **limes**

juice of 2 **lemons**

2 tsp **sea salt**

½ medium **cucumber,** chopped

1 cup (142g) thinly sliced **red onion**

1 cup (142g) diced **Roma** or **plum tomatoes**

½ cup (15g) chopped **fresh cilantro,** plus more to garnish

1 **semi-ripe avocado,** diced

¼ tsp **soy sauce**

extra-virgin olive oil, to finish

tortilla chips, to serve

---

1 Bring a medium pot of salted water to a boil. In a large bowl, prepare an ice bath by combining cold water and ice. Cut the shrimp into ½-inch (1.25cm) chunks. Turn off the heat and poach the shrimp by submerging them in the hot water for 45 seconds, then immediately transfer to the ice bath. Drain.

2 In a large glass or nonreactive bowl, combine the shrimp, lime juice, lemon juice, and salt. Stir well. Cover and refrigerate for 30 minutes to 1 hour, checking for doneness periodically. Shrimp are done when they are fully opaque with no grayish raw parts remaining.

3 Drain the shrimp, reserving the liquid. Return the shrimp to the bowl and add the cucumber, onion, tomatoes, cilantro, avocado, and soy sauce. Toss gently to combine all ingredients.

4 Adjust the seasoning as necessary and add back 3 to 4 tablespoons of the reserved liquid. Transfer the ceviche to a serving bowl and place the bowl over crushed ice to keep it cold. Top with more cilantro and a drizzle of olive oil. Serve with tortilla chips, plantain chips, or whatever else you like.

TIP If you'd like a spicy ceviche, add chopped or diced serrano peppers in step 3.

THAI FISH CURRY

YIELD
6 to 8 servings

PREP TIME
10 minutes

COOK TIME
20 minutes

While a traditional Thai curry takes time and a substantial number of ingredients to properly execute, this recipe is a fantastic way to achieve those bold flavors in considerably less time.

2 tbsp **coconut oil**

1 medium **yellow onion,** divided, half minced and half sliced

2 tbsp minced **fresh ginger**

3 **garlic cloves,** minced

kosher salt, to taste

3 tbsp **Thai red curry paste**

1 tbsp **Brown Sugar** (page 25)

1 (13.5oz [398ml]) can of **full-fat coconut milk**

⅓ cup (80ml) **water**

2 cups (284g) thinly sliced **red bell pepper**

1 cup (142g) chopped **green beans** (1-inch [2.5cm] pieces)

1½lb (680g) **cod** or **halibut,** cut into bite-sized pieces

1 tbsp **fish sauce**

1 tbsp **soy sauce**

juice and zest of 1 **lime**

1 tbsp chopped **fresh cilantro,** plus more to garnish

cooked **white rice,** to serve

chopped fresh **Thai basil,** to garnish

1   In a large pot, heat the coconut oil over medium-high heat. Add the minced onion, ginger, and garlic, and season with salt to taste. Sauté until golden brown, about 5 minutes.

2   Add the curry paste and brown sugar, and cook for 2 to 3 minutes, stirring constantly. Add the coconut milk, water, red bell pepper, green beans, and the sliced onion. Increase the heat to high and bring to a boil for 5 minutes.

3   Reduce the heat to medium-low and add the fish. Cover and cook for 4 minutes or until the fish is just cooked through.

4   Stir in the fish sauce, soy sauce, lime juice and zest, and cilantro. Taste and add salt as needed. Serve over rice, and top with more cilantro and the Thai basil.

TIP   To make this spicy, add finely sliced Thai chiles at the end!

PASTA

LA MIA FAMIGLIA È ITALIANA. OF COURSE I'M GOING TO
HAVE A DEDICATED PASTA SECTION!

SMOKY MEZCAL RIGATONI

YIELD
4 to 6 servings

PREP TIME
5 minutes

COOK TIME
15 minutes

I don't drink alcohol often, but when I do, mezcal is my go-to libation. You'll love this subtle, smoky spin on the classic and undeniably tasty spicy vodka rigatoni.

1lb (454g) **rigatoni**

2 tbsp **extra-virgin olive oil**

3 **garlic cloves,** finely chopped

1 large **shallot,** finely chopped

1½ tsp **red pepper flakes**

½ cup (116g) **tomato paste**

⅓ cup (80ml) **mezcal**

¾ cup (180ml) **heavy cream**

1½ cups (150g) freshly grated **Parmesan cheese,** plus more to garnish

½ tsp **smoked paprika**

smoked salt, to taste

1   Bring a large pot of salted water to a boil over high heat. Cook the rigatoni according to the package directions. While the pasta cooks, prepare the sauce.

2   In a large skillet over medium heat, combine the olive oil, garlic, shallots, and red pepper flakes. Cook for about 1 minute, stirring constantly. Stir in the tomato paste and cook for 1 minute more.

3   Remove the skillet from the heat and add the mezcal. When bubbling subsides, return the skillet to medium heat and, if you desire, tilt the pan toward the flame to flambé. Be careful, as this may create a large flame. Let the pan sit as the flame burns out.

4   Once the flame dissipates, stir in the cream and Parmesan. Add the smoked paprika and season with smoked salt to taste. Slowly whisk in some of the pasta water, ¼ cup (60ml) at a time, until you reach your desired consistency. Remove the skillet from the heat and allow the sauce to rest, which will help bring out the vibrant orange color.

5   When the rigatoni is done cooking, drain the pasta and add it to the sauce. Toss to combine. Finish with more grated Parmesan before serving.

HOW TO FLAMBÉ

YOLKY GNOCCHI

YIELD
3 servings

PREP TIME
25 minutes

COOK TIME
1 hour 15 minutes

If you make this for a first date, I can practically guarantee a second.

2lb (900g) **russet potatoes**
  (about 4 medium potatoes)

1 large **egg**

¾ cup (90g) **all-purpose flour,**
  plus more for dusting

pinch of **kosher salt**

freshly grated **nutmeg,** to taste

3 tbsp **high-heat cooking oil**

3 small **egg yolks**

⅓ cup (51g) **Browned Butter**
  (page 41), warmed

freshly grated **Parmesan cheese,**
  to taste

TIP   Weigh your potatoes and flour to ensure a perfect ratio. After ricing, you should have 1 pound (454g) of potato.

1   Preheat the oven to 400°F (200°C). Poke each potato about 8 times with a fork. Bake on a parchment-lined baking sheet for 60 to 75 minutes or until tender. Remove from the oven and cool slightly, just until they are no longer too hot to handle.

2   Working quickly, remove the potato skins and use a potato ricer to rice the potatoes into a medium bowl. (The potatoes must be warm to incorporate the flour.) Using a fork, gently stir in the whole egg, then sprinkle in the flour and distribute it evenly throughout the potato mixture. Add a pinch of salt and grate a small bit of nutmeg across the potato dough.

3   Lightly flour a work surface and knead the dough for 1 minute or until smooth, dusting with flour as needed to prevent sticking. Roll the dough into a long, uniform log about ½ inch (1.25cm) thick. Using a knife or bench scraper, cut the log into ½-inch (1.25cm) segments, then pinch the edges of each segment so they look like small pillows. Using a bench scraper, transfer the gnocchi to 2 parchment-lined baking sheets, spacing them out.

4   Bring a large pot of salted water to a boil over high heat. Lift the parchment paper from one of the pans and gently slide the gnocchi into the pot. Once they float, count slowly to 30 before removing them. Total cook time will be 3 to 4 minutes.

5   While the first batch of gnocchi boils, heat the oil in a large nonstick skillet over medium-high heat. Using a slotted spoon or spider, add the cooked gnocchi directly to the hot pan. (Be careful; the hot oil will splatter at first.) Cook, untouched, for 3 minutes or until each pillow of gnocchi gets a light golden brown crust on one side. Repeat with the remaining gnocchi.

6   Divide the gnocchi evenly among 3 plates and arrange into small nests. Add an unbroken raw egg yolk to the center of each nest. Spoon the hot browned butter over the top and sprinkle with Parmesan. Just before serving, break the yolk and mix with the browned butter to create a nutty, flavorful sauce.

HOW TO PRONOUNCE
"GNOCCHI"

FRENCH + ITALIAN LASAGNA

YIELD
8 servings

PREP TIME
20 minutes

COOK TIME
1 hour 45 minutes

This dish couples the classic Italian lasagna components (pasta, cheeses, and ragù) with a French béchamel sauce, which adds a transformative creaminess to the dish.

1lb (454g) **Fresh Ricotta** (page 37)

2 cups (100g) freshly grated **Parmesan cheese**, divided

½ cup (57g) shredded **mozzarella**

½ tsp **dried oregano**

½ tsp **dried parsley**

kosher salt, to taste

1 tbsp **extra-virgin olive oil**, for greasing

1¼lb (567g) **lasagna noodles** or 1 batch **Pasta Dough** (page 42), rolled and cut into sheets

FOR THE RAGÙ

2oz (57g) raw **bacon**, chopped

1 **yellow onion**, finely chopped

1 **celery stalk**, finely chopped

1 **carrot**, finely chopped

4 **garlic cloves**, minced

2 tsp **kosher salt**

2 tbsp **tomato paste**

1½lb (680g) **ground Italian sausage**

1½lb (680g) **ground pork**

1 cup (240ml) **dry white wine**

1 (28oz [794g]) can of **crushed tomatoes**

FOR THE BÉCHAMEL

¼ cup (57g) **unsalted butter**

¼ cup (30g) **all-purpose flour**

3 cups (720ml) **whole milk**

pinch of freshly grated **nutmeg**

kosher salt and freshly ground **black pepper**, to taste

1 To make the ragù, in a large Dutch oven, cook the bacon over medium heat for 4 to 5 minutes, stirring occasionally, until golden brown. Add the onion, celery, carrot, garlic, and salt. Cook for 6 to 7 minutes, stirring occasionally. Add the tomato paste and cook for 2 minutes more. Add the sausage and pork, and cook for 6 to 8 minutes until lightly browned, breaking up the meat as you stir.

2 Increase the heat to medium-high and add the wine. Cook for about 5 minutes or until most of the liquid has evaporated. Add the tomatoes. Continue to simmer, uncovered, for at least 1 hour and up to 4 hours as you finish the remaining steps, adjusting the temperature as needed to continue thickening the ragù.

3 To make the béchamel, in a large saucepan, melt the butter over medium-low heat. Add the flour and whisk to remove any clumps. Cook until the mixture begins to slightly bubble but doesn't brown, 1 to 3 minutes. Add ¼ cup (60ml) of milk and whisk until smooth. Add the remaining milk. Increase the heat to medium and whisk until the mixture reaches a low boil. Continue whisking for 3 to 4 minutes more or until the mixture thickly coats the back of a spoon.

4 Taste and season with a pinch of nutmeg, salt, and pepper. Transfer the mixture to a large bowl. Cover with plastic wrap and refrigerate until ready to use.

5 Preheat the oven to 350°F (175°C). In a medium bowl, combine the ricotta, 1 cup of the Parmesan, mozzarella, oregano, parsley, and salt to taste. Pour in the béchamel and lightly fold together until just combined.

6 Lightly brush a 9 × 13-inch (23 × 33cm) glass or ceramic baking dish with the olive oil. Coat the bottom of the dish with a very thin layer of ragù and top with a layer of lasagna noodles (uncooked; they will cook as the lasagna bakes). Continue by layering ⅓ of the ragù, ½ of the béchamel–ricotta mixture, and another layer of noodles, then repeat once more. Finish by topping with the remaining ragù and sprinkling the remaining 1 cup of the Parmesan over the top. Cover the dish with foil and bake for 45 minutes.

7 Remove the dish from the oven and take off the foil. Preheat the oven to broil (high). Return the dish to the oven and broil for about 5 minutes until the surface becomes golden brown and bubbly, rotating for even browning if necessary. Allow the lasagna to rest for a few minutes before serving.

FANCY RAMEN
TWO WAYS

Here we have an easy and oddly perfect pesto ramen and an accessible carbonara that uses bacon instead of the classic Italian guanciale—though if you can find guanciale, I'd highly recommend using it instead!

YIELD
Pesto: 2 servings
Carbona(ra)men: 2 servings

PREP TIME
Pesto: 2 minutes + making pesto
Carbona(ra)men: 5 minutes

COOK TIME
Pesto: 2 minutes
Carbona(ra)men: 10 minutes

FOR THE PESTO RAMEN

2 (3oz [85g]) packages of **ramen noodles** (noodles only; discard the seasoning packet or reserve for another use)

⅔ cup (150g) **Roasted & Toasted Pesto** (page 45)

⅓ cup **toasted pine nuts**

fresh basil (optional), to garnish

freshly grated **Parmesan cheese** (optional), to garnish

FOR THE CARBONA(RA)MEN

8 slices of **bacon,** cut into ½-inch (1.25cm) pieces

2 cups (480ml) **water**

2 (3oz [85g]) packages of **ramen noodles** (noodles only; discard the seasoning packet or reserve for another use)

½ cup (70g) **frozen peas**

3 large **egg yolks,** whisked

¾ cup (75g) freshly grated **Parmesan cheese**

¾ cup (75g) freshly grated **Pecorino Romano cheese**

kosher salt and freshly ground **black pepper,** to taste

PESTO RAMEN

1   Fill a large saucepan halfway with water and bring to a boil over high heat. Add the ramen and cook for 2 to 3 minutes or until al dente. (It will likely take less time than the package instructions recommend.)

2   Drain, reserving some pasta water, and transfer the ramen to a large bowl. Stir in the pesto and a splash of pasta water, if needed. Sprinkle the pine nuts over the top before serving, along with fresh basil and Parmesan, if desired.

CARBONA(RA)MEN

1   In a large skillet, cook the bacon over medium-high heat for 10 to 12 minutes or until the fat has rendered. Transfer the cooked bacon to a plate lined with paper towels, leaving behind the rendered fat.

2   Add the water to the skillet with the rendered fat. Bring to a boil over medium-high heat. Add the ramen and peas, and cook for 2 to 3 minutes or until al dente. Midway through cooking, reserve 1 cup (240ml) of pasta water and set aside to cool.

3   When most of the liquid has evaporated, turn off the heat and stir in the egg yolks, Parmesan, Pecorino, and bacon. Stir to combine, adding the reserved pasta water as needed. A perfect sauce should coat the noodles. Season with salt and pepper to taste before serving.

RICOTTA RAVIOLI
WITH LEMON SAUCE

YIELD
4 to 6 servings

PREP TIME
30 minutes + making pasta dough

COOK TIME
20 minutes

When asked my favorite thing to cook, ravioli always comes to mind. It's truly enjoyable to prepare, despite the labor that goes into it. That first bite makes it all worthwhile.

1lb (454g) **Fresh Ricotta** (page 37), drained

1 cup (100g) freshly grated **Parmesan cheese**

¼ tsp freshly grated **nutmeg**

½ tsp **lemon zest**

kosher salt and freshly ground **black pepper**, to taste

1 **egg yolk**

1 tbsp **water**

1 batch **Pasta Dough** (page 42)

FOR THE SAUCE

4 tbsp **unsalted butter**

1 **garlic clove**, minced

2 tbsp **all-purpose flour**

⅓ cup (80ml) **dry white wine**

zest and juice of 1 **lemon**, plus more to serve

½ cup (120ml) **heavy cream**

2 **egg yolks**

kosher salt and freshly **ground black pepper**, to taste

1 cup (100g) freshly grated **Parmesan cheese**, to garnish

chopped **fresh chives** (optional), to garnish

1. In a medium bowl, combine the ricotta, Parmesan, nutmeg, lemon zest, and salt and pepper to taste. Once you feel it's properly salted, add just a pinch more.

2. In a small bowl, combine the egg yolk and water to make an egg wash. Mix well and set aside.

3. Divide the pasta dough into 4 equal portions. Using a pasta maker, roll out 1 portion of dough on the second-to-last setting (5–6mm thickness), and cut it to create 2 pasta sheets of equal size. Working quickly, place the 2 sheets next to one another on a work surface. Using 2 spoons, distribute the ricotta filling in small, evenly spaced mounds across one of the pasta sheets, about 1 to 1½ tablespoons of filling per mound.

4. Using a pastry brush, quickly brush the dough around each mound of filling as well as the top of each mound with the egg wash, then place the second sheet of pasta on top and press around each edge to seal. Try to avoid creating air bubbles.

5. Using a knife or ring mold, cut the dough into ravioli shapes. (If cutting into rounds, discard the excess dough.) Place the ravioli on a lightly floured surface and cover with a kitchen towel to prevent drying. Repeat the process of rolling and filling with the remaining portions of pasta dough. It's important to work quickly in small batches to prevent the dough from drying out. You should create 20 to 25 2-inch (5cm) ravioli in total.

6. Bring a large pot of salted water to a boil over high heat. Working in batches if needed, add the ravioli and cook for about 3 minutes or until they float to the surface. Drain, reserving about 1 cup (240ml) of pasta water, and set aside.

7 To make the lemon sauce, in a large skillet over medium-high heat, melt the butter. Add the garlic and sauté for 1 minute, stirring often. Reduce the heat to medium and sprinkle in the flour. Whisk for 1 to 2 minutes, making sure not to brown the mixture. Add the wine, lemon juice, and lemon zest. Whisk for 1 minute more.

8 Add the cream and ¾ cup (180ml) of pasta water, plus more as needed. Cook, whisking until you get a smooth consistency and the sauce thickens, about 3 minutes.

9 Remove the skillet from the heat and stir in the egg yolks. Season with salt and pepper to taste. Add the cooked ravioli to the pan and very gently toss to coat fully in the sauce.

10 Transfer the ravioli to serving plates. Sprinkle with the Parmesan and grate additional lemon zest over the top. Garnish with the chives, if using.

SHRIMP SCAMPI

YIELD
4 servings

PREP TIME
15 minutes

COOK TIME
25 minutes

The name "shrimp scampi" is laughably redundant—it essentially translates to "shrimp shrimp." If a recipe has shrimp TWICE in its name, you'd better make sure to get that maximum shrimpy flavor.

3 tbsp **kosher salt,** plus more to taste

2 tbsp **granulated sugar**

1½lb (680g) **shell-on jumbo shrimp,** shells and tails removed and reserved

2 tbsp **extra-virgin olive oil,** divided

1½ cups (360ml) **dry white wine**

4 sprigs **fresh thyme**

4 tbsp **unsalted butter**

6 **garlic cloves**, thinly sliced

2 medium **shallots**, finely diced

½ tsp **red pepper flakes**

freshly ground **black pepper**, to taste

8oz (227g) **linguine**

2 tbsp freshly squeezed **lemon juice,** plus **lemon zest** to serve

½ tsp **cornstarch**

⅓ cup (8g) chopped **fresh parsley**

crusty bread, to serve

TIP If you can get head-on shrimp, this recipe tastes even better. Whether they're head-on or head-off, look for high-quality shrimp that haven't been treated with preservatives.

1   To a medium bowl, add 4 cups (960ml) of cold water and whisk in the salt and sugar. Add the shrimp and cover with plastic wrap. Refrigerate while you measure out and prepare the remaining ingredients, no longer than 15 minutes. Pat the shrimp dry with paper towels and set aside. Discard the soaking liquid.

2   In a large skillet, heat 1 tablespoon of olive oil over high heat until it shimmers. Add the shrimp shells (and heads, if you were lucky enough to get them) and sauté for 3 to 4 minutes, stirring often, until they darken in color. Turn off the heat and add the wine and thyme sprigs. After stirring for about 30 seconds, turn the heat back to medium and cook for 5 minutes.

3   Strain the wine mixture over a medium bowl, then set the liquid aside and discard the solids. Prepare a large pot of salted water over high heat for cooking the linguine.

4   To the same pan over medium heat, add the remaining 1 tablespoon of olive oil and the butter. When the butter melts, add the garlic, shallots, red pepper flakes, and salt and black pepper to taste. Cook, stirring occasionally, for 3 minutes or until the garlic is fragrant. Add the shrimp and sauté for 2 to 3 minutes, then remove and set aside. Add the wine mixture, reduce the heat to low, and allow it to simmer while you cook the pasta.

5   In the large pot of salted boiling water, cook the linguine for 8 minutes. When the pasta is almost done, in a small bowl, combine the lemon juice and cornstarch and whisk it into the wine mixture, bringing it to medium heat.

6   Using tongs, immediately transfer the pasta to the wine mixture, reserving the pasta water. Turn the heat to high and cook for 1 to 2 minutes or until the pasta is fully cooked. Add about ½ cup (120ml) of the pasta water to ensure there is enough sauce to coat all the pasta evenly. It should be nice and saucy!

7   Add the shrimp, then stir once more and divide evenly among individual serving plates. Finish with parsley and lemon zest, and serve with crusty bread.

SUNGOLD SPAGHETTI

YIELD
4 to 6 servings

PREP TIME
10 minutes

COOK TIME
20 minutes

While exploring the farm from which Chef Michael Tusk sources ingredients for his Michelin three-star restaurant Quince, I tasted a few Sungold tomatoes straight from the vine. They're sweet and sugary, with a light tartness that balances them out. He helped create a recipe that highlights these wonderful gifts from nature.

4 cups (500g) **Sungold cherry tomatoes,** divided

2 **garlic cloves,** divided

1 tsp **white wine vinegar**

1 tsp + a pinch of **kosher salt,** divided

½ cup (120ml) **extra-virgin olive oil,** plus more to garnish

½ cup (75g) sliced **red onion**

¼ cup (50g) jarred **cherry peppers,** deseeded and sliced

1lb (454g) **thick spaghetti**

⅔ cup (67g) freshly **grated Parmesan cheese,** divided

1 tsp chopped **fennel fronds,** divided

2 tsp chopped fresh **purple basil** or **regular basil,** divided

1 tsp **marjoram,** fresh or dried, divided

1 Bring a large pot of salted water to a boil over medium-high heat. While the water boils, continue with the next steps.

2 Cut 2 cups (250g) of the tomatoes in half from stem to end. Mince 1 garlic clove. In a medium bowl, combine the halved tomatoes, minced garlic, white wine vinegar, and a pinch of salt. Gently mash with a fork until the juices are released. Set aside.

3 Thinly slice the remaining garlic clove. In a large sauté pan, heat the olive oil over medium heat until warm. Add the onion, cherry peppers, sliced garlic, and 1 of teaspoon salt. Cook for about 5 minutes, stirring occasionally, until tender. Add the tomato–garlic mixture to the pan and cook for 2 to 3 minutes more, then remove from the heat and set aside.

4 To the pot of boiling water, add the spaghetti. Cook for about 8 minutes, 2 to 3 minutes less than instructed on the package. Using tongs, immediately transfer the pasta to the cherry tomato sauce, reserving the pasta water.

5 Return the sauté pan to medium heat and add about 1½ cups (360ml) of pasta water, stirring constantly. Add the remaining 2 cups (250g) of cherry tomatoes and cook for 3 to 4 minutes to slightly soften the tomatoes and thicken the sauce.

6 Add half the Parmesan and toss to combine. Taste and season with salt if needed. Add half of the fennel, basil, and marjoram, and toss.

7 Divide the pasta evenly among individual serving plates and garnish with the remaining herbs, the remaining Parmesan, and a light drizzle of olive oil.

FETTUCCINE CACIOFREDO

YIELD
4 to 6 servings

PREP TIME
5 minutes

COOK TIME
15 minutes

Chicken parm, spaghetti and meatballs, alfredo sauce . . . they may be delicious, but they don't exist in Italy. To pay homage to my Italian-American roots, I combined the beautiful elements of *cacio e pepe, pasta al burro,* and *fettuccine alfredo* to create the king of all cream pastas.

1lb (454g) **fettuccine**

¾ cup (128g) **Browned Butter** (page 41)

1 cup (240ml) **heavy cream**

1½ tsp **kosher salt**

½ tsp freshly ground **black pepper**

½ cup (50g) freshly grated **Parmesan cheese**

½ cup (50g) freshly grated **Romano cheese**

chopped **fresh parsley,** to garnish

---

1 Bring a large pot of salted water to a boil over medium-high heat. Add the fettuccine and cook for 8 minutes or until al dente. (If using fresh pasta, cook for about 3 minutes or until the pasta begins to float to the surface.)

2 While the pasta cooks, in a large saucepan, heat the butter and cream over low heat. When the butter has melted, add the salt and pepper. Increase the heat to medium and add about ½ cup (120ml) of the pasta water and both cheeses, whisking until the cheeses have melted and the sauce thickens. This only takes a few minutes; the sauce should be thickened by the time the pasta is done cooking.

3 Using tongs, transfer the cooked pasta straight from the pot into the sauce. Mix until fully coated, adding more pasta water if needed to thin out the sauce.

4 Serve immediately on slightly warmed plates and garnish with parsley.

TIPS   To change it up and make a more complete meal out of this recipe, add sliced cherry tomatoes or broccoli florets to the butter before adding the cream in step 2.

To reheat leftovers, add about a tablespoon of water and mix it into your pasta, then either heat in the oven or microwave.

CARBS

YOUR BRAIN NEEDS THEM.
YOUR HEART WANTS THEM EVEN MORE.

GRILLED PIZZA "AL FORNO"

YIELD
3 10-inch (25cm) pizzas

PREP TIME
15 minutes

COOK TIME
25 minutes

My first restaurant job was in Providence, Rhode Island. The restaurant, Al Forno, is known as the "birthplace of grilled pizza." It's the best pizza I've ever had. This is a spinoff I created with my friend Andris, who eats, sleeps, and breathes pizza.

1lb (454g) pre-made **pizza dough**

all-purpose flour, for dusting

high-heat cooking oil, for greasing

1 cup (113g) freshly grated **Fontina cheese**

⅔ cup (67g) freshly grated **Romano cheese**

½ cup (50g) freshly grated **Parmesan cheese**

1 (14.5oz [425g]) can of whole **San Marzano tomatoes**

kosher salt, to taste

¾ cup (20g) **fresh basil,** chopped

¾ cup (20g) **fresh flat-leaf parsley,** chopped

extra-virgin olive oil, to finish

6 **scallions,** thinly sliced

1   Divide the dough into 3 equal portions, each about 5⅓ ounces (150g), and place on a lightly floured baking sheet. Cover with plastic wrap and rest at room temperature until needed.

2   Oil the grill grates and preheat the grill to 400°F (200°C).

3   In a medium bowl, lightly mix the Fontina, Romano, and Parmesan cheeses until evenly combined. Set aside.

4   Add the tomatoes (with juices) to a large bowl. Using your hands, crush the tomatoes into a slightly chunky purée. Add a pinch of salt. Set aside.

5   On a lightly floured work surface, use a rolling pin to roll out 1 ball of dough as thinly as possible, using flour as necessary to keep the dough from sticking to your hands or the work surface. You want an extremely thin crust, as it will puff up a lot when it cooks.

6   When the grill is hot and oiled, use your fingertips to gently lift the dough and drape it onto the grill. Cook for 1 to 2 minutes or until grill marks appear. Using tongs, flip the dough.

7   Working quickly, brush the dough with olive oil and sprinkle evenly with ⅓ of the grated cheese mixture. Use a spoon to add several large dollops of tomatoes across the dough. Sprinkle some of the basil and parsley over the top of the dough. Close the grill lid and cook for 4 to 5 minutes or until the cheeses have melted.

8   Remove the pizza from the grill. Drizzle a little olive oil over the top and sprinkle a healthy dose of raw scallions over the pizza before serving. Repeat steps 6 to 8 with the remaining dough and toppings.

PIZZA DOUGH RECIPE

CRISPY ROASTED POTATOES

YIELD
6 to 8 servings

PREP TIME
10 minutes

COOK TIME
35 to 40 minutes

English roasted potatoes are known for having a crispy exterior and a light, fluffy interior. In other words, they're the perfect roasted potatoes. My recipe follows a rather classic method, with the unique addition of mayonnaise—my secret ingredient for the world's butteriest potatoes.

2lb (907g) **Yukon Gold potatoes**

1 tbsp **kosher salt**

¼ tsp **baking soda**

2 tbsp melted **clarified butter**

⅓ cup (75g) **mayonnaise**

Homemade Flaky Salt (page 22) and freshly ground **black pepper,** to taste

1 Preheat the oven to 450°F (230°C). Line a large baking sheet with parchment paper. Peel the potatoes and cut them into bite-sized chunks.

2 Fill a large pot ¾ full with water and bring to a boil over high heat. When boiling, stir in the kosher salt and baking soda. Add the potatoes (the water should cover them), return to a boil, and then reduce the heat to maintain a low simmer. Simmer for 10 to 15 minutes or until the potatoes are fork-tender. Drain the potatoes and transfer to a large bowl.

3 Pour the clarified butter over the potatoes and add the mayonnaise. Using a rubber spatula, stir the potatoes and rough up the edges, creating more surface area and therefore more crispiness. The exteriors of the potatoes should begin to get a bit mushy. Spread the potatoes evenly on the prepared baking sheet.

4 Place the baking sheet in the oven and roast the potatoes for 15 to 20 minutes. Check for browning and continue roasting for up to 10 minutes or until they reach your desired crispiness.

5 Remove from the oven and finish with flaky sea salt and pepper.

TIPS Baking soda draws the starch to the surface of the potatoes, ultimately making them crispier.

You can also make these in an air fryer! Follow the same general steps, shaking the basket every so often until they're golden brown and crispy.

PAPA'S CRISPY RICE

YIELD
8 servings

PREP TIME
20 minutes

COOK TIME
1 hour 30 minutes

My grandfather was born in Tehran, Iran—home of *tahdig,* or golden crispy rice. Although he rarely cooked, he did make the best rice of anybody I've ever met, which we lovingly called "Papa Rice." I've adapted his method in favor of an easier, oven-baked version.

2 cups (400g) **basmati rice**

¼ cup (57g) **unsalted butter,** melted

½ tsp finely ground **saffron threads** (optional)

⅓ cup (75g) **plain yogurt**

1 large **egg yolk**

¼ cup (60ml) **grapeseed** or **canola oil**

1 Bring a large pot of generously salted water to a boil over high heat. In a large fine-mesh strainer, rinse the rice under cold water until the water runs clear.

2 Add the rice to the boiling water. Cook for 5 to 6 minutes and then begin checking for doneness. Each grain of rice should be soft around the edges and firm in the center (not fully cooked). Drain in a fine-mesh strainer, shaking to remove as much water as possible, and then spread the rice on a baking sheet to dry.

3 Place a rack in the lower third of the oven and preheat the oven to 400°F (200°C). Generously grease a 9-inch (23cm) glass pie dish with the butter. In a small bowl, combine the saffron (if using) and 2 teaspoons of hot water. Steep for 10 minutes.

4 To the bowl with the saffron, add the yogurt, egg yolk, and oil, and stir to combine. Stir in 2 cups (340g) of the parboiled rice and mix thoroughly to ensure every grain of rice is coated.

5 Transfer the yogurt–rice mixture to the prepared dish, pressing it firmly into the bottom. Top with the remaining rice and cover tightly with foil.

6 Place in the oven and bake until the rice is golden brown on the bottom and slightly up the sides, anywhere from 65 to 85 minutes. After 1 hour, begin peeking at the underside of the glass dish to gauge the browning.

7 Remove from the oven and cool for several minutes, then place a large plate upside down over the pie dish and—in one confident motion—flip them both over. Serve immediately.

HOW TO FLIP A TAHDIG

CAST-IRON NAAN

YIELD
8 flatbreads

PREP TIME
30 min + 1 hour to rise

COOK TIME
15 minutes

First of all, please don't ever, EVER call it "naan bread." That's like saying "pesto sauce" or "chai tea." It's naan. And second, they say naan can't be done without a tandoor (clay oven), but they haven't tried this recipe.

½ cup (120ml) **warm water**

1 tsp **granulated sugar**

2¼ tsp **active dry yeast**

2¼ cups (270g) **all-purpose flour**

½ cup (114g) **plain yogurt**

½ tsp **kosher salt**, plus more to taste

1 tbsp **extra-virgin olive oil**, plus more for greasing

3 tbsp **unsalted butter**, melted

2 sprigs of **fresh cilantro**, chopped

1 In a large bowl, whisk together the water and sugar. While whisking, gradually add the yeast. Let sit for about 5 minutes or until the yeast activates and becomes foamy.

2 Add the flour to the bowl, then stir in the yogurt, salt, and oil. Once loosely mixed together, transfer to a clean work surface. Knead until the surface is smooth and shiny. This should take about 10 minutes.

3 Place the dough in a lightly greased bowl and cover with a damp kitchen towel. Place the dough in a warm location to rise until doubled in size, about 1 hour.

4 Divide the dough into 8 equal portions. Using a rolling pin, roll each portion into an 8-inch (20cm) round.

5 Heat a large cast-iron skillet over medium-high heat. Lightly brush one side of a round of dough with water. Add the dough to the skillet, wet side down, and cover the skillet with a lid. Cook for about 1 minute until the dough puffs and a few charred spots appear. Flip and cook on the other side, uncovered, for 1 minute more. Remove the naan from the skillet and repeat with the remaining portions of dough.

6 As you remove the hot naan from the skillet, use a pastry brush to brush each one with melted butter, then sprinkle salt and a little chopped cilantro over the top of each one before serving.

TIP Covering the skillet immediately after adding the dough will lead to a lighter, puffier texture. There's no need to cover after flipping.

VELVETY MASHED POTATOES

YIELD
10 to 12 servings

PREP TIME
15 minutes

COOK TIME
40 minutes

While I'm not saying there's a right or wrong way to enjoy your mashed potatoes (as with peanut butter, I have my opinions on chunky vs. creamy, but I won't judge), I do have a few tips that will ensure a better, creamier final product.

4lb (1.8kg) **Yukon Gold potatoes**

3 tbsp + 4 tsp **kosher salt,** divided

1 cup (240ml) **whole milk**

½ cup (120ml) **heavy cream**

1 head of **garlic,** unpeeled, cut in half horizontally

3 sprigs of **fresh rosemary**

1 cup (226g) **unsalted butter,** cubed

chopped **fresh chives,** to garnish

freshly ground **black pepper,** to garnish

TIP A chinois is a great kitchen gadget to own because you can use it to strain purées, soups, and sauces. It also comes in handy for dusting powdered sugar over the top of a decadent dessert.

1 Peel the potatoes and place them in a large bowl of cool water after peeling to prevent oxidation.

2 Transfer the potatoes to a large pot. Cover the potatoes with cold water. Add 3 tablespoons of kosher salt to the pot, then bring to a boil over high heat. Reduce the heat to low and simmer for 30 to 35 minutes until the potatoes are fork-tender.

3 Drain and rinse the potatoes under cool water to remove any excess starch. Return the potatoes to the warm, dry pot and cover with a kitchen towel. The residual heat will allow them to steam while you prepare the remaining ingredients.

4 In a small saucepan, combine the milk, heavy cream, garlic, and rosemary. Simmer over medium heat for 5 minutes or until fragrant. Remove the saucepan from the heat and set aside.

5 Into a large bowl, pass the hot potatoes through a potato ricer. Do this when they're still as hot as possible. Add the butter and the remaining 4 teaspoons of salt. Using a rubber spatula, stir until the butter has melted. Slowly strain the warm milk mixture through a chinois (or the finest mesh strainer you have) into the potatoes. Stir until fully incorporated.

6 Before serving, sprinkle with chives and black pepper.

BRAZILIAN CHEESE BALLS

YIELD
24 balls

PREP TIME
20 minutes

COOK TIME
15 to 20 minutes

Once a year during college after finishing our midterm exams, my roommates and I headed to an all-you-can-eat Brazilian steakhouse to splurge on dinner. Secretly, I didn't go for the meat. Instead, I saved room for the *pão de queijo*— the cheesy and gooey cheese balls that were endlessly brought to the table.

unsalted butter, for greasing

¼ cup (60ml) **whole milk**

¼ cup (60ml) **water**

½ tsp **kosher salt**

½ cup (170g) **Browned Butter** (page 41)

2 cups (226g) **tapioca flour**

2 large **eggs**

½ cup (50g) freshly grated **Parmesan cheese**

¼ cup (28g) shredded **mozzarella**

1 Preheat the oven to 400°F (200°C). Grease a mini muffin tin with butter.

2 In a large pot over medium-high heat, combine the milk, water, salt, and browned butter. Bring the mixture to a boil and then remove the pot from the heat.

3 In the bowl of a stand mixer fitted with a paddle attachment, combine the milk mixture and tapioca flour. Mix on medium speed until a sticky dough begins to form.

4 Add the eggs, one at a time, and mix until fully incorporated. Add the Parmesan and mozzarella, and mix until well combined. The dough should be slightly sticky. Using a rounded tablespoon, spoon the dough into the prepared muffin tin, dividing it evenly among the wells. (A second spoon may be useful to scrape the sticky dough from the tablespoon into the muffin tin.)

5 Bake for 15 to 20 minutes or until the cheese balls puff up to the size of golf balls and become golden brown. Serve immediately.

FLOUR TORTILLAS

YIELD
6 7-inch (15cm) tortillas or
4 10-inch (25cm) tortillas

PREP TIME
15 minutes + 30 minutes to rise

COOK TIME
5 minutes

Every Tuesday is "Taco Tuesday" in my house. I can promise that making your own tortillas is as easy as it is delicious.

2 cups (240g) **all-purpose flour,** plus more for dusting

1¼ tsp **table salt**

¼ tsp **baking powder**

⅓ cup (75g) **lard** or softened **unsalted butter**

⅔ cup (160ml) **lukewarm water**

1   In a medium bowl, whisk together the flour, salt, and baking powder.

2   Add the lard or softened butter and mix with a fork until the mixture becomes crumbly.

3   Add the water and use a rubber spatula to mix until a sticky dough forms.

4   Transfer the dough to a floured work surface and knead for 1 to 2 minutes.

5   Divide the dough into 4 to 6 pieces of equal size (fewer if you want larger tortillas; more if you want smaller tortillas). Roll each into a ball, then cover with a kitchen towel for 30 minutes.

6   On a floured work surface, use a rolling pin to roll out each ball as thinly as possible, aiming to keep each one perfectly circular.

7   Heat a large skillet over medium heat. Once hot, cook each tortilla in the dry pan for about 30 seconds on each side. The tortilla will develop golden brown charred spots and puff up in some areas; do not pop the air bubbles as they form.

8   Remove the tortilla from the skillet and use immediately or store for later use. Tortillas can be stored in an airtight container for 2 to 3 days at room temperature, up to 1 week in the refrigerator, and much longer in the freezer.

TIP   To prevent your fresh tortillas from drying out before serving, cover them with a kitchen towel or place them in a foil pouch until ready to eat. This will keep them fresh and soft.

24-HOUR FOCACCIA

YIELD
8 to 10 servings

PREP TIME
15 minutes + 24 hours to rest dough

COOK TIME
20 to 30 minutes

Focaccia is an incredibly well-rounded bread—full of surface area for a crispy exterior, fluffy and airy on the inside, and dimpled to easily hold any toppings. And with this recipe adapted from *Bon Appétit*, there's no need to knead!

2½ cups (600ml) **lukewarm water**

2½ tsp **honey**

2¼ tsp **active dry yeast**

5 cups (600g) **all-purpose flour**

1 tbsp **kosher salt**

5 tbsp **extra-virgin olive oil**, plus more for drizzling

unsalted butter, for greasing

Homemade Flaky Salt (page 22)

1 sprig of **fresh rosemary**, leaves stripped from the stem

2 tbsp **Browned Butter** (page 41)

TOPPINGS (OPTIONAL)

chopped **fresh herbs**

Roasted & Toasted Pesto (page 45)

cured meats

TIP Although you can make this recipe in just a few hours if you're truly pressed for time, it's not quite the same in terms of flavor and airiness.

LiFTiNG THE DOUGH iN THE BOWL

1 In a large bowl, whisk together the water, honey, and yeast. Let sit for 5 minutes to ensure the yeast activates and becomes foamy. Add the flour and kosher salt. Mix with a rubber spatula until a shaggy dough forms.

2 To a separate large bowl, add the olive oil, then add the dough and turn it around to coat in oil. Cover the bowl with plastic wrap and refrigerate for 24 hours or up to several days. If you're pressed for time, you can allow the dough to rest at room temperature until doubled in size, about 3 to 4 hours.

3 Generously grease a 9 × 13-inch (23 × 33cm) baking pan (or a rimmed baking sheet, depending on the thickness of focaccia you prefer) with unsalted butter. Set aside.

4 Using two forks, lift the dough from the edges of the bowl toward the center of the bowl. (Scan the QR code for instructions.) Continue doing this until you've gone around the whole bowl three times.

5 Transfer the dough to the prepared pan, including any residual oil, and lightly spread the dough to fill the edges of the pan. Allow to rise again, uncovered, in a warm area for 1½ to 3 hours.

6 Place a rack in the middle of the oven and preheat the oven to 450°F (230°C).

7 Carefully stretch and adjust the dough as needed to reach the edges of the pan. Use your fingers to add dimples to the dough, about every inch or so. (This is my favorite part about making focaccia.) Drizzle a little olive oil over the surface of the dough and sprinkle with homemade salt and rosemary.

8 Bake for 20 to 30 minutes or until golden brown to your liking. Remove the pan from the oven and brush with browned butter. Drizzle with more olive oil, and top with herbs, pesto, or cured meats, if desired.

SALADS
+ VEGGIES

EAT YOUR VEGETABLES. WITH THE RIGHT TECHNIQUES,
EVEN BRUSSELS SPROUTS CAN BE A STAR.

RANCH WEDGE SALAD

YIELD
4 servings

PREP TIME
5 minutes + making croutons, dressing, and bacon

COOK TIME
12 to 18 minutes

During the cookbook shoot, our photographer Max accidentally knocked over this salad, shattering the plate and making a mess on the floor. It reminded me of Massimo Bottura's purposeful "Oops! I dropped the lemon tart" masterpiece, so we picked it up and took a picture. A wedge salad isn't supposed to look neat, anyway.

1 cup (42g) **Garlicky Croutons** (page 46)

4 slices of **prosciutto**

2 cups (480g) **high-heat cooking oil,** for frying

⅓ cup (40g) **capers**

1 head of **iceberg lettuce,** quartered

1 cup (264g) **Ranch Dressing** (page 48)

⅓ cup (38g) **blue cheese crumbles** (optional)

4 strips of **Maple & Lemon Bacon** (page 79), chopped

1 small **red onion,** minced

2 small **tomatoes,** diced and salted

2 tbsp chopped **fresh chives**

kosher salt and freshly ground **black pepper,** to taste

1. In a food processor, pulse the croutons into a coarse breadcrumb-like consistency.

2. To crisp the prosciutto, preheat the oven to 375°F (190°C) and place the prosciutto on a parchment-lined baking sheet. Bake for 10 to 15 minutes, then set aside to cool.

3. In a large saucepan, heat the oil over high heat to 350°F (175°C). Add the capers and fry for 2 to 3 minutes or until they break open and crisp up. Transfer to a plate lined with a paper towel.

4. To assemble each salad, place 1 lettuce wedge on a plate. Drizzle ¼ cup of dressing over the lettuce and add the blue cheese crumbles (if using).

5. Add the breadcrumbs, bacon, fried capers, onion, tomatoes, and chives to the plate. Break the crispy prosciutto into shards and crumble over the top. Season with salt and pepper to taste before serving.

MISO EGGPLANT

YIELD
4 servings

PREP TIME
10 minutes

COOK TIME
15 minutes

Eggplant is underrated. It often seems boring—until it's not. One of the best dishes I've ever had was a miso eggplant dish at a Japanese restaurant. This recipe serves as a reminder of the day I saw the true potential of eggplant.

2 small **eggplants**

2 tbsp **high-heat cooking oil**

¼ cup (80g) **white miso paste**

2 tbsp **mirin**

1 tbsp **granulated sugar**

1 tsp minced **fresh ginger**

1 tbsp **sake** or **white wine**

TO GARNISH

chopped **scallions**

toasted **sesame seeds**

lime or **lemon wedges**

toasted sesame oil

TIP   Smaller eggplants are typically less bitter, a little sweeter, and more tender. Choose wisely at the grocery store or farmers market. For an even better result, use Japanese eggplants—they're a bit harder to find but more tender and delicious.

1 Preheat the oven to 375°F (190°C). Line a baking sheet with foil.

2 Slice each eggplant in half lengthwise and use a paring knife to score the cut sides, making a small crisscross pattern without cutting through the skin.

3 In a large nonstick skillet, heat the oil over high heat. Add the eggplant skin side down. Cook for 2 to 3 minutes or until the skins turn golden brown.

4 Gently flip the eggplant, then lower the heat to medium. Cover the skillet with a lid and cook for 4 to 5 minutes or until the flesh is fork-tender.

5 Meanwhile, in a small bowl, combine the miso paste, mirin, sugar, ginger, and sake.

6 Place the eggplant skin side down on the prepared baking sheet. Using a pastry brush, coat the flesh with half the miso glaze. Place the sheet in the oven and bake for 3 to 5 minutes or until light golden brown and tender.

7 Remove the sheet from the oven and brush the eggplant with the remaining miso glaze. Preheat the oven to broil.

8 Return the sheet to the oven and broil for 2 to 3 minutes or until the surface is golden brown.

9 Transfer the eggplant to a serving platter. Sprinkle the scallions and sesame seeds over the top. Before serving, squeeze lime juice over each eggplant half and drizzle with sesame oil.

GRILLED PEACHES + BURRATA

YIELD
2 to 4 servings

PREP TIME
10 minutes

COOK TIME
5 to 10 minutes

The best recipes are those that are easy and make you look like a pro. Sweet, charred peaches combined with creamy burrata make for the ultimate eating experience.

2 medium ripe **peaches,** cut into sixths

1 tbsp **unsalted butter,** melted

1 tbsp **granulated sugar**

2 tbsp **balsamic glaze**

8oz (227g) **burrata cheese**

2 tbsp **extra-virgin olive oil**

¼ cup (35g) **toasted pine nuts**

Homemade Flaky Salt (page 22), to taste

freshly ground **black pepper,** to taste

fresh basil, to garnish

1 Preheat the grill to high heat. (You can also heat a cast-iron grill pan over medium-high heat on the stovetop.)

2 Using a pastry brush, coat the peach slices with the butter and sprinkle the sugar on both sides.

3 Place the peaches on the grill and cook for 3 to 5 minutes per side or until the peaches are slightly soft and grill marks appear. Remove the peaches from the grill and set aside.

4 Create an artistic swirl of the balsamic glaze on a large serving plate. Have fun with it! Tear the burrata into several large hunks and arrange the cheese around the plate.

5 Evenly distribute the grilled peach slices around the burrata hunks. Top the peaches and cheese with the olive oil, pine nuts, basil, and salt and pepper to taste before serving.

TIPS If you want to be extra fancy, find some truffle burrata or substitute the olive oil with truffle oil.

If peaches are out of season, you can substitute thawed frozen peaches, but use a cast-iron grill pan instead of a grill, as they can stick easily.

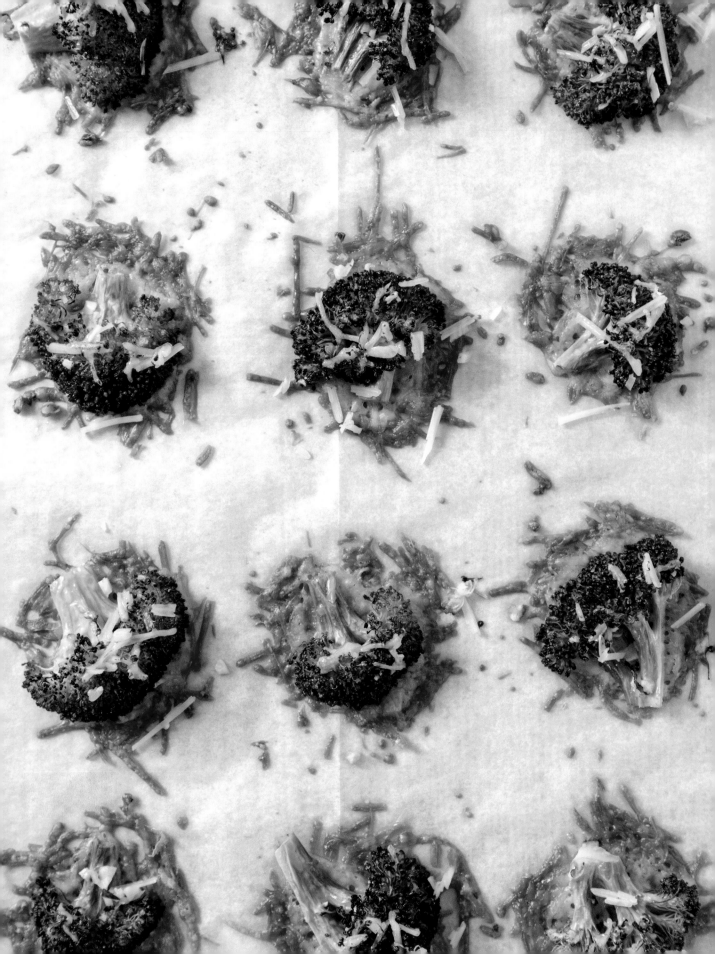

PARMESAN ROASTED BROCCOLI

YIELD
4 servings

PREP TIME
10 minutes

COOK TIME
15 minutes

If you've ever tasted one of those Parmesan crisps, you know how good they are. Combine that concept with crispy roasted broccoli and you've got yourself a winner that will convert even the biggest broccoli hater.

1½ cups (150g) finely grated
   Parmesan cheese, divided
6 cups **broccoli florets,** each
   floret cut with a flat side
¼ cup (60ml) **extra-virgin olive oil**
4 **garlic cloves,** minced
kosher salt and freshly ground
   black pepper, to taste
zest and juice of 1 **lemon,** to taste

1   Preheat the oven to 400°F (200°C). Line a baking sheet with parchment paper.

2   Distribute 1 cup (100g) of the grated Parmesan across the prepared baking sheet in small piles, about 2 teaspoons each (roughly the size of a broccoli floret).

3   In a medium bowl, toss the broccoli with the olive oil, coating each piece. Add the remaining ½ cup (50g) of Parmesan, along with the garlic, salt, and pepper. Toss until evenly distributed.

4   Place 1 broccoli floret on each Parmesan pile, flat side down.

5   Place in the oven and roast for 15 minutes or until the broccoli is crispy and the cheese on the bottom is golden brown.

6   Remove from the oven, grate some lemon zest over the top, and drizzle with lemon juice, to taste, before serving.

CRISPY BRUSSELS SPROUTS

YIELD
4 servings

PREP TIME
15 minutes

COOK TIME
15 to 20 minutes

For a long time, I couldn't be fooled into eating Brussels sprouts. That is, until I discovered crispy Brussels. The secret to crispy Brussels sprouts is preheating an empty pan in the oven before adding the vegetables to cook. Without this step, the sprouts will overcook before they reach maximum crispiness.

1lb (454g) **Brussels sprouts**

6 tbsp **extra-virgin olive oil**

kosher salt and freshly ground **black pepper,** to taste

2 tbsp **balsamic vinegar glaze**

1 tbsp **honey**

1 **lime,** to grate for zest

1   Place an unlined baking sheet in a cold oven. Preheat the oven to 450°F (230°C).

2   While the oven heats, trim off the bottoms of the Brussels sprouts and slice them vertically in half. (Do not wash the Brussels sprouts. Peel off the very outer layer if you want, but washing is unnecessary and will prevent crispiness. Rough them up a little bit and peel back some of the leaves to get them extra crispy.)

3   Carefully remove the hot pan from the oven and add the oil. Moving quickly and carefully, arrange the sprouts cut side down in the pan, ensuring each one is placed on some oil and that they're evenly spaced to prevent overcrowding. Season with salt and pepper to taste.

4   Return the pan to the oven and roast for 15 to 20 minutes or until the sprouts are crispy and golden brown on the bottom.

5   Remove the pan from the oven and transfer the sprouts to plates or a serving bowl. Before serving, drizzle on the balsamic vinegar glaze and honey, and grate some lime zest over the top.

PERSIAN STREET CORN

YIELD
6 servings

PREP TIME
15 minutes

COOK TIME
4 to 5 minutes

"Persian" and "street corn" aren't often mentioned together, but here, they mesh beautifully. This recipe combines the lemony twist of the Persian spice sumac with creamy, delicious Mexican-style street corn.

½ cup (57g) **Cotija,** plus more to garnish

¼ cup (57g) **mayonnaise**

¼ cup (57g) **sour cream**

¼ cup (7g) chopped **fresh cilantro**

1 tbsp **ground sumac,** plus more to garnish

½ tsp **kosher salt**

juice and zest from 1 **lime**

6 ears of **fresh sweet corn,** shucked

Homemade Flaky Salt (page 22), to garnish

1 Preheat the grill to maximum heat. (You can also broil or cook on an open oven flame if necessary.)

2 In a small bowl, stir together the Cotija, mayonnaise, sour cream, cilantro, sumac, kosher salt, and lime juice. Set aside.

3 Place the corn on the grill and char for 4 to 5 minutes or until charred to your liking.

4 Transfer the corn to a serving platter. Coat each ear of corn evenly with the mayonnaise mixture, and sprinkle generously with more Cotija, more sumac, lime zest, and flaky salt.

GREEN GODDESS CUCUMBERS

YIELD
2 servings

PREP TIME
12 minutes

COOK TIME
none

Green goddess dressing tastes great on everything, but it pairs particularly well with cucumbers for a crunchy, creamy, and refreshing salad.

5 to 6 **Persian cucumbers**

kosher salt and freshly ground **black pepper,** to taste

1 **lemon,** to grate for zest

extra-virgin olive oil, to finish

⅓ cup (16g) chopped fresh **chives**

1 tbsp **toasted sesame seeds**

FOR THE DRESSING

1 tbsp freshly squeezed **lemon juice**

¾ cup (168g) **mayonnaise**

¼ cup (57g) **sour cream**

¼ cup (6g) chopped **fresh parsley**

1 tbsp **tarragon leaves**

1 small **garlic clove**

1 Slice the cucumbers as you prefer. I like to accordion slice them. (Scan the QR code for instructions.)

2 In a large bowl, toss the cucumbers with salt and pepper to taste. Allow the cucumbers to sit to draw out their flavors.

3 To make the dressing, in a blender, combine the lemon juice, mayonnaise, sour cream, parsley, tarragon, and garlic. Blend on high until smooth.

4 When ready to serve, drain the cucumbers in a fine mesh strainer to remove any excess water. Transfer to a serving dish and drizzle the dressing over the cucumbers. Before serving, grate some lemon zest over the top, drizzle on a bit of olive oil, and sprinkle with the chives and sesame seeds.

TIPS   Persian cucumbers are the small ones that often come in packs of five or six. They're far more flavorful than conventional cucumbers.

This recipe makes about 1⅓ cups (330g) of dressing—save any leftover dressing for dipping veggies!

HOW TO ACCORDION-
SLICE CUCUMBERS

BREADCRUMB CAESAR SALAD

YIELD
4 servings

PREP TIME
15 minutes + making croutons

COOK TIME
none

Caesar has always been my second-favorite salad (behind a good wedge), but I've gotten tired of awkwardly large and sharp—or worse, soggy—croutons.

4 cups (168g) **Garlicky Croutons** (page 46)

1 large **pasteurized egg yolk** (optional)

1 tbsp freshly squeezed **lemon juice**

2 tsp **Worcestershire sauce**

2 tsp **Dijon mustard**

1 tsp **anchovy paste** (optional)

1 **garlic clove,** minced

¼ tsp **kosher salt**

¼ tsp freshly ground **black pepper**

½ cup (120ml) **extra-virgin olive oil**

¼ cup (25g) freshly grated **Parmesan cheese,** plus more to serve

2 **romaine lettuce hearts,** roughly chopped

1 In a food processor, lightly pulse the croutons to create coarse breadcrumbs. (Don't over-blend.) Transfer the breadcrumbs to a small bowl and set aside.

2 In a large bowl, whisk together the egg yolk (if using), lemon juice, Worcestershire sauce, mustard, anchovy paste (if using), garlic, salt, and pepper.

3 Whisking continuously, slowly drizzle in the olive oil until the mixture reaches a thickened dressing consistency.

4 Whisk in the Parmesan. Add the romaine and toss to combine, taking care to coat the lettuce evenly in dressing.

5 Divide the salad among individual serving bowls. Sprinkle each serving with breadcrumbs and additional Parmesan grated with a Microplane grater and shaved with a vegetable peeler to get varying textures.

TIP Use the freshest, crispest lettuce possible for this salad.

SWEETS + TREATS

"WOULD YOU LIKE TO SEE THE DESSERT MENU?"

"NO THANKS, I'LL TAKE THE CHECK."

(AND GO MAKE THEM AT HOME.)

DEVIL'S FOOD CUPCAKES

YIELD
16 cupcakes

PREP TIME
20 minutes

COOK TIME
20 to 25 minutes

When it comes to cupcakes, I like either vanilla cake with chocolate frosting or chocolate cake with vanilla frosting. Mix-matched only. This beautiful chocolate cake base pairs perfectly with the crispy buttercream frosting.

10 tbsp **unsalted butter,** at room temperature

1¼ cups (248g) **granulated sugar**

2 large **eggs**

¾ cup (90g) **cake flour**

¾ cup (90g) **all-purpose flour**

½ cup (42g) **Dutch-processed cocoa powder**

1 tsp **kosher salt**

½ tsp **baking powder**

½ tsp **baking soda**

¾ cup (180ml) freshly brewed **coffee,** cooled to room temperature

¼ cup (60ml) **whole milk**

1 tsp **Aged Vanilla Extract** (page 29)

1 batch **Crispy Buttercream Frosting** (optional; page 238)

1 **lemon** or 1 **orange** (optional), to grate for zest

1 Place a rack in the center of the oven and preheat the oven to 350°F (175°C). Line 2 12-cup muffin tins with 16 cupcake liners.

2 In a stand mixer fitted with a paddle attachment, beat the butter and sugar for 4 to 5 minutes or until light and fluffy. Add the eggs one at a time, beating after each addition until fully incorporated.

3 Into a medium bowl, sift the flours, cocoa powder, salt, baking powder, and baking soda. Whisk until combined. In a separate small bowl, combine the coffee, milk, and vanilla extract.

4 With the mixer running on low speed, alternate adding the coffee mixture and flour mixture, in about three batches, until the batter is smooth and fully combined. Fill each cupcake liner ¾ of the way full.

5 Place the muffin tins in the oven and bake for 20 to 25 minutes or until a toothpick inserted in the middle of a cupcake comes out clean. Start checking after 20 minutes.

6 Remove the tins from the oven and allow the cupcakes to cool completely. Top with the frosting and freshly grated lemon or orange zest, if desired, before serving.

TIP Some people break off the lower portion of their cupcake and place it on top of the frosting to make a sandwich of sorts. I don't know how to feel about it.

BUTTER TOFFEE BARS

YIELD
24 bars

PREP TIME
10 minutes

COOK TIME
30 minutes

My grandmother (of UK origin) has been making these gooey, blondie-like English toffee squares forever—she calls them "brickle bars." I've fully plagiarized her recipe, so Ami, if you're reading this, please don't pursue legal action!

½ cup (113g) **unsalted butter,** softened, plus more to grease the pan

1½ cups (180g) **all-purpose flour**

2 tsp **baking powder**

½ tsp **table salt**

1 cup (198g) **granulated sugar**

½ cup (107g) packed **Brown Sugar** (page 25)

2 large **eggs**

1 tsp **Aged Vanilla Extract** (page 29)

1 (8oz [227g]) bag of **English toffee bits**

1 Preheat the oven to 350°F (175°C). Grease a 9 × 13-inch (23 × 33cm) baking pan with butter.

2 Into a medium bowl, sift the flour, baking powder, and salt. Set aside.

3 In a separate medium bowl or stand mixer, beat the butter, granulated sugar, and brown sugar on medium-high speed until light and fluffy. Add the eggs and vanilla extract. Mix well to combine.

4 Stir the dry ingredients into the wet ingredients. Stir in the English toffee bits. Using a rubber spatula, scrape the batter into the prepared pan and spread evenly.

5 Place the pan in the oven and bake for 30 minutes.

6 Remove the pan from the oven and cool for a few minutes. Cut into bars before serving. They're just as fantastic warm as they are after they've fully cooled and solidified a bit.

BROWNED BUTTER + CHOCOLATE CHIP COOKIES

YIELD
8 large cookies

PREP TIME
15 minutes

COOK TIME
8 to 11 minutes

As a proud Persian, I'm happy to say that the origin of the modern cookie can be traced back to seventh-century Persia. Over 1,000 years later, I've created this recipe that yields large, tall cookies with a crunchy exterior and a gooey interior.

1 cup (170g) cold **Browned Butter** (page 41), cut into cubes

1 cup (213g) **Brown Sugar** (page 25)

½ cup (100g) **granulated sugar**

1 tsp **Aged Vanilla Extract** (page 29)

2 large **eggs**

1 **egg yolk**

1½ cups (180g) **cake flour**

1½ cups (180g) **all-purpose flour**

1 tsp **cornstarch**

¾ tsp **baking soda**

¾ tsp **kosher salt**

8oz (227g) solid **milk chocolate**, broken into chunks

½ cup (85g) **semisweet chocolate chips**

2 cups (226g) **chopped walnuts**

TIP Especially when it comes to cookies, trust your instincts over your timer. We all have our own preferences when it comes to crispiness, gooeyness, and more. This is mine, but I suggest you test to find yours—just don't open the oven too many times in doing so!

1 Preheat the oven to 415°F (210°C). Line a baking sheet with parchment paper.

2 In the bowl of a stand mixer fitted with a paddle attachment, beat the browned butter, brown sugar, granulated sugar, and vanilla extract until well combined, about 4 minutes.

3 Add the eggs and egg yolk one at a time, beating after each addition until fully incorporated.

4 Add the cake flour, all-purpose flour, cornstarch, baking soda, and salt. Mix until just combined.

5 Stir in the chocolate chunks, chocolate chips, and walnuts by hand. The dough will be a bit more crumbly than a typical cookie dough, but if you feel it won't hold together, add 1 to 2 tablespoons of water.

6 Divide the mixture into 8 large mounds and place them on the prepared baking sheet. Make the mounds tall and large, just how you want them to look when they finish. (They don't spread much while baking.)

7 Bake for 8 to 11 minutes or until golden brown. Remove the sheet from the oven and allow the cookies to cool on the baking sheet for at least 10 minutes. Enjoy the cookies while still warm and gooey.

FRUIT LEATHER

Think Fruit by the Foot—but healthier. While this recipe requires some patience, the satisfaction you'll get from peeling and tearing the leather makes it worth the wait.

YIELD
8 strips

PREP TIME
5 minutes

COOK TIME
6 to 8 hours

3 cups (500g) sliced fresh **strawberries**

1 tbsp freshly squeezed **lemon juice**

3 tbsp **honey**

1 Preheat the oven to its lowest setting, ideally between 135°F and 175°F (57–80°C). Line a baking sheet with a Silpat baking mat or parchment paper.

2 In a blender, combine the strawberries, lemon juice, and honey. Blend until smooth, then gently tap the blender on a hard surface to pop any air bubbles. Pour the purée onto the prepared baking sheet and spread thinly and evenly, then slam the sheet on the counter a few times to get it perfectly even. Don't pour too thin of a layer or you'll get thin fruit crisps instead of fruit leather, but don't pour it too thick because it'll take far too long to dry into fruit leather.

3 Place the sheet in the oven and bake for 6 to 8 hours or until the leather is no longer sticky to the touch, but take care not to overcook, as it will become dry and brittle. Start checking at about 3½ or 4 hours because oven temperatures will vary.

4 Remove from the oven and allow the leather to cool completely. Gently peel the leather from the parchment and use a knife to cut it into strips, tear it by hand, or eat it however you'd like!

TIP   Use this method to experiment with other types of fruit leather—I like mango, peach, and blueberry. If you'd like to get fancy, spread two purées of different colors on the baking sheet and swirl to create a beautiful pattern.

HORCHATA

If you've had horchata, you know how great it is. If you haven't, it's a refreshing almond and cinnamon drink made with rice milk.

YIELD
7 cups

PREP TIME
10 minutes + 6 hours to soak

COOK TIME
none

1 cup (200g) uncooked **white rice**, jasmine recommended

1 **cinnamon stick**

½ cup (43g) **slivered almonds**

1 (12oz [340g]) can of **evaporated milk**

⅔ cup (132g) **granulated sugar**, plus more to taste

1 tbsp **Aged Vanilla Extract** (page 29)

1½ cups (360ml) **almond milk**

4¼ cups (1 liter) **water**

1 In a fine-mesh strainer, rinse the rice with cold water until the water runs clear.

2 In a medium bowl, combine the rice, cinnamon stick, and almonds, and add enough water to cover. Let soak for at least 6 hours or overnight, then drain the water.

3 Transfer the rice, almonds, and cinnamon stick to a blender. Add the evaporated milk and the sugar, and blend on high for at least 3 to 5 minutes or until a smooth mixture forms.

4 Strain the liquid through cheesecloth into a large pitcher and add the vanilla extract and almond milk. Mix until well combined, then stir in the water and serve over ice. I like to go back to my childhood days and drink mine through a cinnamon stick.

TIP Evaporated milk is simply milk that's been heated to remove some of the water. It's sweet and creamy. For a dairy-free substitute, use canned sweetened coconut cream.

TANGHULU

I studied Mandarin Chinese throughout high school, and in college, I visited Beijing, where I excitedly flexed my language skills as I ventured through a street food market. After stumbling across this popular sweet treat late one night, I shared it online and people went wild.

YIELD
4 to 5 servings

PREP TIME
5 minutes

COOK TIME
15 to 20 minutes

1lb (454g) **fresh fruit,** such as strawberries, grapes, or mandarin orange segments

2 cups **granulated sugar**

1 cup **water**

1   Line a baking sheet with parchment paper, and prepare an ice bath by combining cold water and ice cubes in a medium bowl. Set both aside.

2   Wash the fruit and thoroughly pat it dry with paper towels. Any moisture on the exterior of the fruit will prevent the sugar coating from sticking. Thread the fruit onto wooden skewers, just 1 to 3 pieces per skewer. Set aside.

3   In a small saucepan, combine the sugar and water. Bring to a boil over medium-high heat.

4   Clip a candy thermometer to the pan and monitor the temperature until it reaches 300°F (150°C), about 15 minutes. If you don't have a candy thermometer, test by dipping a skewer into the sugar mixture and then into the ice bath. If it hardens immediately (not sticky but fully hardened), it's ready.

5   Dip each fruit skewer into the hot sugar mixture and then quickly plunge it into the ice bath to harden. Place on the prepared baking sheet and repeat with the remaining skewers. Serve immediately.

TIP   For the best result, use fruits that don't have a wet, exposed surface. If you want to use a wet fruit (such as sliced mango or kiwi), make sure to dry it as much as possible before dipping.

NO-CHURN NUTELLA ICE CREAM

YIELD
1 quart (1kg)

PREP TIME
15 minutes + 6 hours to chill

COOK TIME
none

No ice cream maker or fancy equipment needed for this recipe! Just easy, at-home ice cream made from simple ingredients.

2 cups (480ml) chilled **heavy cream**

1 cup (240ml) **sweetened condensed milk**

¼ cup (60ml) **whole milk**

1 tbsp **Aged Vanilla Extract** (page 29)

¼ tsp **table salt**

½ cup (148g) **hazelnut cocoa spread** (Nutella recommended), plus more to serve

½ cup (43g) **crumbled toasted almonds** (optional), to serve

1 To a blender, add the heavy cream and blend on low for about 15 seconds. Scrape down the sides with a rubber spatula. Continue blending on medium speed until stiff peaks form, about 30 seconds more, pulsing as needed.

2 Add the condensed milk, whole milk, vanilla extract, and salt. Mix with a whisk or rubber spatula. Pulse again on low speed for about 15 seconds more, scraping down the sides as needed until fully combined. Pour the cream mixture into an 8-inch (20cm) square baking dish.

3 In a small microwave-safe bowl, microwave the hazelnut cocoa spread for 15 seconds or until it has a thinner, pourable consistency. Using a rubber spatula, swirl the cocoa spread through the cream mixture, creating a nice pattern.

4 Cover the pan with plastic wrap, pressing the plastic directly onto the surface of the cream mixture to avoid freezer burn. Freeze until firm, about 6 to 7 hours.

5 To serve, scoop the ice cream into bowls. Drizzle with more thinned cocoa spread, if desired, and sprinkle the crumbled almonds over the top (if using).

GINGERBREAD DOG TREATS

YIELD
36 small dog treats

PREP TIME
25 minutes

COOK TIME
25 to 30 minutes

I'm notorious for naming my pets after foods. I once had a hamster named Pesto and now I have a dog named Pepper. Pepper loves these gingerbread treats. If you don't have a dog but feel so inclined, just make these for yourself.

¼ cup (85g) + 2 tbsp **blackstrap molasses**

½ cup (120ml) + 2 tbsp **water**

¼ cup (60ml) **canola oil**

2 cups (240g) **all-purpose flour**

1 cup (113g) **whole wheat flour**

1½ tsp **ground ginger**

¼ tsp **ground cinnamon**

a pinch of **ground cloves**

1   Preheat the oven to 325°F (165°C). Line a baking sheet with parchment paper.

2   In a large bowl, whisk together the molasses, water, and oil. Mix until well combined.

3   In a medium bowl, whisk together the all-purpose flour, whole wheat flour, ginger, cinnamon, and cloves. Mix until well combined.

4   Add the dry ingredients to the wet ingredients. Use your hands to mix until well combined.

5   Transfer the mixture to a lightly floured surface and knead the dough until smooth. Roll the dough to ¼ inch (0.64cm) thick.

6   Using a bone-shaped cookie cutter (or other cookie cutter), cut the dough into shapes. Place the cutouts on the prepared baking sheet.

7   Place the sheet in the oven and bake for 25 to 30 minutes or until firm.

8   Remove the sheet from the oven and transfer the cookies to a wire rack to cool before serving to your four-legged friends.

TIP   Do not add nutmeg to this recipe. Nutmeg is toxic to dogs!

RECIPES FROM MY FRIENDS

I'VE COLLECTED A FEW RECIPES FROM PEOPLE WHO INSPIRE ME.

CRISPY MAGIC FROSTING

JOANNE CHANG

YIELD
3½ cups (for about 12 cupcakes)

PREP TIME
12 minutes

COOK TIME
5 to 7 minutes

"Crispy magic" buttercream is a mashup of "crispy buttercream" (what you'd typically see in a supermarket) and "magic buttercream" (Swiss meringue buttercream that's magically easy to make). I've combined the two to make what I feel is the ultimate buttercream to frost cakes or to eat by the spoonful. (Seriously! I've seen Nick do it.)

⅔ cup (132g) **granulated sugar**

2 **egg whites**

1½ cups (339g) **unsalted butter,** at room temperature, cut into chunks

1 tbsp **Aged Vanilla Extract** (page 29)

¼ tsp **kosher salt**

1⅔ cups (170g) **confectioners' sugar**

2 tbsp **whole milk**

1 In a small bowl, whisk together the granulated sugar and egg whites to make a thick slurry. Place the bowl over a small saucepan of simmering water, making sure the bottom of the bowl is not touching the water, and heat for 5 to 7 minutes, whisking occasionally, until the mixture is hot to the touch. It will thin out a bit as the sugar melts.

2 Scrape the mixture into the bowl of a stand mixer fitted with a whisk attachment. Beat on medium-high speed for 6 to 8 minutes or until the mixture cools.

3 Add the butter and beat on medium speed until the butter is thoroughly incorporated. The mixture should thicken and then become light and fluffy.

4 Add the vanilla, salt, confectioners' sugar, and milk. Continue to beat on medium until the whole mixture is smooth and satiny.

5 Transfer the frosting to an airtight container. Store at room temperature for up to 3 days or in the fridge for up to 2 weeks. Before using, place the frosting in the bowl of a stand mixer fitted with the paddle attachment and remix until the frosting smooths out again.

HOT HONEY LEMON PEPPER WINGS

THE GOLDEN BALANCE

YIELD
4 servings

PREP TIME
5 minutes

COOK TIME
20 minutes

Nick and I were casually experimenting in the kitchen one day and made these. After taking the first bite, we stopped chewing and excitedly turned to each other. These wings are truly something special!

high-heat cooking oil, for frying

2lb (907g) **chicken wings**

2 tbsp **Cajun seasoning**

6 tbsp **unsalted butter**

2 tbsp freshly ground **black pepper**

¼ cup (84g) **hot honey**

1 **lemon**, to grate for zest

1 In a large Dutch oven, heat 3 to 4 inches of oil to 375°F (190°C) over high heat.

2 In a large bowl, combine the chicken wings and Cajun seasoning. Mix with your hands to ensure the wings have been thoroughly coated.

3 Working in batches, add the wings to the hot oil, taking care not to crowd the pan. Fry until the wings are golden brown and reach an internal temperature of 180°F (80°C), about 8 to 12 minutes, depending on the size of the wings.

4 In a small saucepan, melt the butter over medium heat. Add the pepper and toast for 2 to 3 minutes or until aromatic. Stir in the hot honey and immediately remove from the heat.

5 Transfer the wings to a large bowl and add the sauce. Toss to coat. Before serving, use a Microplane grater to grate some lemon zest over the top.

ASPARAGUS + PARMESAN RISOTTO

KEN ORINGER

YIELD
5 to 6 servings

PREP TIME
5 minutes

COOK TIME
35 minutes

This risotto is a popular dish I make at the beginning of asparagus season every year. The addition of miso and Parmesan give the ultimate umami boost, resulting in a final product that has a perfect balance of creamy, cheesy, and earthy.

6 cups (1.4 liters) **Rotisserie Chicken Stock** (page 34)

2 bunches of thick **asparagus,** trimmed and cut into ¼-inch (7mm) segments, divided

8 tbsp **unsalted butter,** divided

1 large **yellow onion,** diced

3 **garlic cloves,** minced

2 cups (200g) **carnaroli** or **arborio rice**

2 tbsp **white miso paste**

½ cup (120ml) **white wine**

¾ cup (75g) freshly grated **Parmesan cheese,** plus more to garnish

2 tbsp chopped **fresh mint**

zest of 1 **lemon,** plus more to garnish

3 tbsp **extra-virgin olive oil**

kosher salt and freshly ground **black pepper,** to taste

3 tbsp **coconut oil,** melted

1   In a large pot, bring the chicken stock to a simmer over medium-high heat. Add half the asparagus and cook for 2 to 3 minutes or until tender.

2   Using a slotted spoon, transfer the cooked asparagus to a blender. Add 1½ cups (360ml) of the warm chicken stock. Blend until smooth. Stir the mixture into the pot of stock. Reduce the heat to low and maintain a low simmer as you prepare the remaining ingredients.

3   In a large sauté pan, melt 3 tablespoons of butter over medium heat. Add the onion and sauté for 4 to 5 minutes or until soft. Add the garlic and sauté for 1 to 2 minutes more. Add the rice and stir to coat. Add the miso paste and stir to combine. Add the white wine and cook, stirring continuously, until the wine has evaporated and the mixture is dry, about 2 to 3 minutes.

4   Add the asparagus stock one ladle at a time, stirring continuously after each addition. Each time the liquid has absorbed, add another ladle of stock. Continue this process until all the stock has been used. The rice should be al dente.

5   Stir in the Parmesan, mint, lemon zest, and the remaining 5 tablespoons of butter. Remove from the heat and set aside.

6   In a separate large sauté pan, heat the olive oil over medium-high heat. Add the remaining asparagus and sauté for 4 to 5 minutes or until al dente. Season with salt and pepper to taste.

7   Divide the risotto evenly among individual serving plates and top with the asparagus. Drizzle the coconut oil over the top and garnish with additional Parmesan and lemon zest.

COMPOST COOKIES

LYNN (LYNJA) DAVIS

YIELD
16 cookies

PREP TIME
15 minutes + 1 hour to chill

COOK TIME
18 minutes

With this "kitchen sink" creation, you can empty your pantry of all the random scraps and bits to make fun and delicious cookies.

2¼ cups (270g) **all-purpose flour**

1 tsp **baking soda**

1 tsp **kosher salt**

1 cup (226g) **Browned Butter** (page 41), softened

1 cup (213g) packed **Brown Sugar** (page 25)

½ cup (100g) **granulated sugar**

2 medium **eggs**

1 tsp **Aged Vanilla Extract** (page 29)

¾ cup (100g) **sweet mix-ins**, such as candy-coated chocolate, toffee bits, chocolate chips, rainbow sprinkles, etc.

¾ cup (100g) **savory mix-ins**, such as crushed potato chips or pretzels, nuts, ground coffee, etc.

1 In a medium bowl, whisk together the flour, baking soda, and salt. Set aside.

2 In the bowl of a stand mixer fitted with the paddle attachment, combine the browned butter, brown sugar, granulated sugar, eggs, and vanilla. Beat on medium-high speed for 3 minutes.

3 Lower the mixer speed and slowly add the flour mixture. Mix until just combined, about 30 seconds.

4 Add the sweet mix-ins. Mix until just incorporated. Add the savory mix-ins and mix for 30 seconds.

5 Line 2 baking sheets with parchment paper. Using a 2¾-ounce scoop, scoop the dough onto the prepared baking sheets. Cover with plastic wrap and refrigerate for at least 1 hour.

6 Arrange the oven racks in the middle and top positions. Preheat the oven to 325°F (165°C).

7 Place the sheets in the oven and bake for 18 to 20 minutes or until golden brown, switching the position of the two sheets halfway through. Remove from the oven and allow the cookies to cool and set slightly before serving

TIPS Store the cookies in an airtight container with a slice of white bread to keep them fresh longer.

Unbaked cookies can be frozen on a baking sheet, transferred to a freezer bag for storage, and baked from frozen in a 325°F (165°C) oven for 20 to 22 minutes.

SOFT PRETZELS

ROBERT IRVINE

Growing up around so many great British pubs, I became a sucker for a pub pretzel. Serve with your favorite stone-ground mustard or beer cheese sauce—and enjoy!

YIELD
6 pretzels

PREP TIME
30 minutes + 40 minutes to rise

COOK TIME
15 minutes

1½ cups (360ml) + 1 tbsp **warm water,** divided

1 tbsp **granulated sugar**

2 tsp **kosher salt**

2¼ tsp **active dry yeast**

4½ cups (540g) **all-purpose flour**

¼ cup (57g) **unsalted butter,** melted

vegetable oil spray, for greasing

1 large **egg yolk**

⅔ cup (146g) **baking soda**

1–3 tsp **pretzel salt,** to taste

cheese sauce or **mustard** (optional), to serve

1. In the bowl of a stand mixer fitted with a dough hook, combine 1½ cups (360ml) of warm water, sugar, kosher salt, and yeast. Let sit for 5 to 10 minutes or until the mixture starts to foam.

2. Add the flour and butter. Begin to mix on low. After all the flour has been incorporated, increase the speed to medium and continue to knead until all the ingredients are incorporated and the dough is in one lump. It will be a bit moist and sticky.

3. Transfer the dough to a work surface and knead into a ball. Lightly oil a medium bowl with vegetable oil spray. Place the dough in the bowl and cover with plastic wrap. Allow the dough to rise for about 40 minutes or until doubled in size.

4. Preheat the oven to 450°F (230°C). Line a baking sheet with parchment paper. In a small bowl, whisk together the egg yolk and 1 tablespoon of water to make an egg wash. Set aside.

5. Divide the dough into 6 balls of equal size and roll each ball into a long rope. Form each rope into a pretzel shape.

6. Fill a large pot with 10 cups of water and add the baking soda. Bring to a boil over high heat. Working in batches as needed, carefully lower the pretzels into the boiling water and cook for about 45 seconds, flipping once midway.

7. Using a small strainer, gently lift the pretzels out of the water and place on the prepared baking sheet. Using a pastry brush, brush the pretzels with the egg wash. Sprinkle the pretzel salt over the top.

8. Place the sheet in the oven and bake for about 12 minutes or until the pretzels are golden brown.

9. Remove the sheet from the oven and serve the pretzels hot or allow them to cool slightly. Serve with cheese sauce or mustard, if desired.

BEEF, BEET + CABBAGE BORSCHT

ANDREW ZIMMERN

YIELD
8 servings

PREP TIME
30 minutes

COOK TIME
3 hours 30 minutes

This was all I ever wanted to eat growing up. I still crave it more than I care to admit. This cabbage soup is technically more of a shchi than a borscht, but why quibble over names? I've been making it for decades, so it's a battle-tested classic.

2 tbsp **vegetable oil**

3lb (1.4kg) **English-cut beef short ribs**

8 cups (1.9 liters) **beef stock**

1 cup (240ml) **dry red wine**, divided

½ tbsp **juniper berries**

½ tbsp **whole black peppercorns**

½ tbsp **whole coriander seeds**

2 sprigs of **fresh dill**

2 sprigs of **fresh oregano**

2 sprigs of **fresh flat-leaf parsley**

2 tbsp **unsalted butter**

3 **beets**, peeled and diced

1 small **rutabaga**, peeled and diced

1 **leek**, thinly sliced

1 small **yellow onion**, diced

1 **carrot**, diced

2 **celery stalks**, diced

1lb (454g) shredded **savoy cabbage**

½ (14oz [397g]) can of **chopped tomatoes**, juices included

2 tbsp **red wine vinegar**

kosher salt and freshly ground **black pepper**, to taste

TO SERVE (OPTIONAL)
sour cream
chopped **fresh dill**
grated **horseradish**

1 In a large heavy pot, heat the oil over medium heat. Add the short ribs and cook until browned all over, about 5 minutes. Add the stock and ½ cup (120ml) of the wine and then bring to a boil. Cover, reduce the heat to low, and simmer for 2 hours or until the meat is very tender.

2 Transfer the short ribs to a baking sheet and allow them to cool. Strain the broth through a fine-mesh strainer and reserve. Discard the bones. Remove and discard the connective tissue. Dice and reserve the remaining meat.

3 Wrap the juniper berries, peppercorns, coriander seeds, dill, oregano, and parsley in a double layer of cheesecloth and tie tightly into a bundle.

4 In the same pot, melt the butter over medium heat. Add the beets, rutabaga, leek, onion, carrot, celery, cabbage, and the herb and spice bundle. Cook until the vegetables begin to soften and the cabbage has wilted, about 15 minutes, stirring occasionally. Add the tomatoes and the remaining ½ cup (120ml) of wine, and simmer for 2 minutes. Stir in the strained broth and simmer until the vegetables are tender, about 1 hour.

5 Stir in the vinegar and the chopped meat, then simmer for 15 minutes more. Season with salt and pepper to taste.

6 Serve the borscht with sour cream, chopped fresh dill, and grated horseradish, if desired.

ACKNOWLEDGMENTS

I could fill this entire book with the names of people I'd like to thank. You are one of them. None of this would have happened without your support, and I am profoundly grateful for each and every person reading this. I wish I could shake each of your hands personally or give you a warm plate of food, but for now, this will have to do.

I'm a firm believer that nothing in life happens without family. Thank you to my amazing parents who've supported me endlessly. And to my three younger brothers, Cam, Pete, and Will, who constantly push me to keep moving, whether they know it or not. And our gentle, loyal dog Leo. To my extended family for inspiring me in the kitchen in so many ways. And to Isabelle, who is such a supportive partner, always by my side. To my late hamster Pesto and my dog Pepper, for loving human food just as much as the rest of us. And to my close friends and fellow social media creators—all of you know who you are.

They say dishwashers are the unsung heroes of any kitchen. This is true. A major thanks to my good friend Sidnei and his entire cleaning team. I know you had great practice cleaning Julia Child's kitchen back in the day (seriously!), but even that couldn't have possibly prepared you for what a kitchen looks like after one makes a 3,000-pound sushi roll.

Thank you to my agent, Mahzad, for always having my back. Brandi, my literary agent, for bringing this book to fruition. And to my incredible team—I've listed you all alphabetically here (sorry, Zach): Brandon, Cole, Jeremy, Joelle, Keevan, Kevin, Manny, Maroua, Ryan, Tim, and Zach. I am inspired by the passion and creativity each of you brings to work each day—and I think we can all agree that we're beyond lucky to do what we do.

And of course, the team at DK and Penguin Random House: Ann, Becky, Chris, Mike, and the entire marketing team. And those who worked tirelessly alongside me on perfecting the recipes and capturing such stunning photos: Ashley, Elizabeth, Judean, Manya, Max, and Shari.

And finally, to Gordon for believing in me and all that I'm working so hard to achieve. I realize that none of this—the cookbook nor my current career in the culinary world—may have happened without you, so thank you.

Thank you all so much.

INDEX